TO YOUR HEALTH!

TO YOUR HEALTH!

THE **BEER DOCTOR** ON GOOD BEER, GOOD TIMES, AND THE FINER THINGS IN LIFE

BY CAROL A. WESTBROOK, MD, PhD

LITTLE
PLUM
PRESS

Little Plum Press
Beverly Shores, IN 46301

Copyright © 2014 by Carol A. Westbrook, MD, PhD

All rights reserved. No part of this publication may be reproduced, distributed, or transmitted in any form or by any means, including photocopying, recording, or other electronic or mechanical methods, without the prior written permission of the publisher, except in the case of brief quotations embodied in critical reviews and certain other noncommercial uses permitted by copyright law.

First printing 2014
Printed in the United States of America
18 17 16 15 14 13 12   1 2 3 4 5

Designed by Laurie Douglas

Photo credits:
Jeff Lloyd, So Many Roads Photography, front cover and page 87; Dolli Quattrocchi Gold, back cover; Chester Garstki, opposite page 1 (top); Cecilia Garstki, opposite page 1 (bottom); Carol Westbrook, page 23 (top), 49, 119, 148, 155, 164, and 172; Richard Rikoski, page 23 (bottom), 70 (family album), 96, 109, and 178; Jason Rhee, page 137.

ISBN-13: 978-0692239957 (Little Plum Press)
ISBN-10: 0692239952

CONTENTS

INTRODUCTION		v
CHAPTER 1:	Beer and the Doctor	1
CHAPTER 2:	The Basics: Lessons in Beer Styles and Ingredients	26
CHAPTER 3:	Beer and Your Health	52
CHAPTER 4:	Our Regional Beers: Northeastern Pennsylvania	71
CHAPTER 5:	Regional Beers from Other Areas	97
CHAPTER 6:	Beer Pairings	114
CHAPTER 7:	Cooking with Beer	149
CHAPTER 8:	Other Spirits	160
AFTERWORD		174
ABOUT THE AUTHOR		178

INTRODUCTION

"To your health!" Almost every nation has a similar salutation when sharing a drink with others. "To your health!" "To life!" "Salute!" We drink together to celebrate life, health, friendship, and good times. When shared with friends, a good beer makes us forget our troubles and our ailments, and it helps us to remember only our good times together.

"*Na zdrowie*" is the Polish translation of "To your health." I heard this phrase a lot as a child because drinking beer was as natural as drinking water in the Polish-American community where I grew up. But that did not make me an expert on beer. In fact, I started writing *The Beer Clinic*—the blog that is the basis for this book—quite by accident.

I had just started home brewing, and my good friend Paul Ciminero assumed this meant that I had special knowledge about beer. He recommended me to his longtime friend Harvey Gold, who had just started the online zine YourBeerNetwork.com, saying I should become a contributor.

At first I balked, but then I thought, why not? I had degrees in medicine and biochemistry, I understood brewing (or so I thought), I knew something about health, and—like most doctors—I wasn't afraid to express my opinions.

And I liked beer.

But I was not interested in merely writing reviews about beers. For me, sharing a beer is about good health, good times, and good friendship—not just good beer. Thus, *The Beer Clinic* was born.

My first article as the Beer Doctor was published on YourBeerNetwork.com on January 1, 2011. At that time, craft beer was a rare commodity, and one might have had to travel a long way to find a bar or restaurant that served anything other than mass-market beer. But over the last three years, craft beer has become more available, due in part to increased production—the number of craft breweries is at its highest since 1890. The Brewers Association reported that in 2013, there were 2,347 craft breweries in the United States, including 1,132 brewpubs, 1,118 microbreweries, and 97 regional craft breweries—producing 6.5 percent of the volume of the total American beer market!

Craft beer is also in high demand by consumers, due to its increased recognition, which is driven in part by beer-aficionado sites like YourBeerNetwork.com. Craft beer has really taken off—people want to know more about it and how it fits into their daily living.

I have been writing for YourBeerNetwork.com for three years now, which is as long as it takes to complete a medical residency—the process of becoming a proficient physician. When I began writing for the site, I was an inexperienced amateur brewer and a full-time clinician in a sleepy Indiana town that had very few good beer bars. Since then, I have written more than 30 articles about beer, moved to a more beer-rich area in Northeastern Pennsylvania, and home-brewed over a dozen batches—one of which won a local award.

I've made many new friends, including some bartenders, brewers, and even teetotalers. I've written a book about cancer and have taken care of many cancer patients, including some survivors. I've learned a thing or two about beer and even more about life.

And that's what *The Beer Clinic* is about—the experience of life, as reflected in beer. The pages that follow are a compendium of three years of my writings as the Beer Doctor. In the same spirit, I am also including a few articles that were published elsewhere. I've taken a few liberties by revising or updating some of the articles, though I've kept the place names and beer names intact. I am not presenting the articles in the order they were published, but I have grouped them into related topics.

Since this book is published on paper and I'm limited to black-and-white, I've had to omit most of the colorful images and online layout created by our talented web designer, Dolli Gold. I'd like to thank her, and I'd also like to thank my online editor, Harvey Gold, for his support.

INTRODUCTION

I also thank my partner in crime, Paul Ciminero, who invariably drags me to the best places when we are in Chicago together. He is now publishing his own blog/podcast site, *TransmusicAirwaves.podomatic.com*. I thank my son and daughter-in-law, Gene Westbrook and Annie Tasker, for their assistance with several beer-tasting projects. And I am grateful to my husband, Rick, who has spent many patient hours helping me taste at breweries, bars, and restaurants—both locally and around the world.

I hope you enjoy reading this compilation as much as I enjoyed writing the articles. From *The Beer Clinic* to you, reader, here's to your health!

Carol at age three.

Carol's father, Chester Garstki, at the backyard grill in July 1976. Note the champagne glass in hand and the bottles on the ground.

CHAPTER 1

BEER AND THE DOCTOR

As you can surmise, this chapter is autobiographical—covering my life from childhood, through medical school, on to my university faculty days, and finally, to my life as it is now, in clinical practice.

The unifying theme is beer and good spirits. This is not to imply that alcohol is a central part of my life—it isn't—but merely to illustrate how spirits are such an integral part of the human experience. There are some good yarns—and good memories—shared with friends over a beer or two.

WHY I DRINK BEER

YourBeerNetwork.com (January 1, 2011)

I'm a doctor and I drink beer.

I drink beer because I like it, because I'm fascinated by it, and because it's OK to drink beer.

Yes, I drink other alcoholic beverages, but I have a special fondness in my heart for beer. My attraction to beer has been attributed to my Polish ancestry (100 percent Polish on both my parents' sides). But I think I would have become a beer drinker regardless of my ancestry, because I really and truly just like the taste of beer.

I am always surprised to find people who don't like beer. To me, beer is a wonderfully natural, refreshing beverage that has been enjoyed by humans for as long as we have been cultivating our own food crops. Who couldn't love it? Yes, there are folks who don't like beer because they don't—or can't—drink alcohol, and there are a few people who can't drink beer because of allergies to hops or grain. But I take issue with people who claim they dislike beer but have only tasted mass-produced, beer-flavored beverages such as *Budweiser*. That's like saying you don't like seafood when you've only eaten fish sticks and have never tasted lobster.

Now I'm not trying to convince a wine aficionado that beer is better or to convert someone who is dead-set against beer that he or she must take it up. But I'd like to reach people who are interested in learning about (and tasting) more beer and who want to deepen their appreciation of it. For these folks, we have *The Beer Clinic*.

What does being a doctor have to do with beer?

Although I am a beer amateur, I also have a medical degree as well as a PhD in biochemistry. This gives me a unique perspective that lets me really understand the complex chemistry of beer and appreciate its health effects.

You probably already know that beer is produced from barley flavored with hops. But let's be more precise: beer is a beverage produced by the alcoholic fermentation of sugars that are derived from malting of the starches contained in cereal grains, usually flavored with hops. Let's break this down and see what we can learn.

ALCOHOLIC FERMENTATION OF SUGARS

Fermentation is the process of yeast breaking down sugars into ethanol and carbon dioxide. Primitive farmers probably learned early on that any sweet liquid left for a few days would turn into a marvelous drink with intoxicating properties: alcohol. Yet if this delicious liquid were not drunk immediately, it would soon become sour and lose its intoxicating properties. You may have inadvertently learned this on your own when you let an old container of apple cider or orange juice sit in the back of your refrigerator, only to find it had turned into vinegar.

CHAPTER 1: BEER AND THE DOCTOR

Sweet liquids were not easy to come by in prehistoric, subsistence-farming communities, but they included honey (producing mead) and fruit (producing cider or other fruity alcohols). The recognition that sprouted grain was sweet no doubt led to attempts to ferment it as well—and beer was the pleasant result.

Where does the yeast come from? No problem—wild yeasts are everywhere. Leave out an open container of sweet liquid and airborne wild yeasts will soon find their way to it. And if you get a particularly good fermentation product—either beer, wine, cheese, or bread dough—you can save the yeast and reuse it, eventually producing a strain of brewer's yeast. Some of these strains are closely guarded and highly prized, and they contribute to the unique characteristics of the beers they produce.

How do you stop vinegar from forming? There are only three ways:

1. Keep the beer cold. This worked well for farmers in northern climates, but not in the south. This is undoubtedly why beer making was refined to a high art in northern European countries but never developed much in the south, where wine grapes were a more convenient source of fermentable sugars.

2. Keep oxygen out of the beer. This is how we do it today. Ethanol is derived from sugar and contains two carbon atoms and one oxygen atom, so if oxygen is available, it will combine with the ethanol (with the help of yeast or bacteria) and produce acetic acid—or vinegar. If there is no oxygen present, there will be no vinegar. So we keep the fermentation vessel closed, let the carbon dioxide build up to drive off the oxygen, and pop the cork once in a while to let off pressure.

3. The heck with it—just drink up the beer when it's ready. This is no doubt what happened in the early (prehistoric) years of beer production. When the brew was ready, you

drank it! Perhaps that's the origin of Oktoberfest and other beer festivals throughout the world. Beer drinking has always been a social event.

SUGARS DERIVED FROM MALTING STARCHES

Cereal grains are seeds, of course, and starch is a form of stored energy for the seed to use when it starts to grow. Starch consists of sugar molecules chemically joined to each other. You cannot ferment starches. Neither can starches be used as an energy source for the developing plant when the seed is planted.

But nature helps us out. As soon as the seed is wet and ready to sprout, enzymes break down the starch into sugars to produce what is called malted grain. It took an astute farmer to realize that his wet grain was not spoiled but had instead turned into a highly sweet liquid, like fruit juice or honey, that could be fermented. If you have the opportunity to do any home brewing, you will have a chance to taste malt extract, which is extremely sweet and resembles honey or corn syrup more than it resembles grain.

CEREAL GRAINS

Just about any grain can be used to make beer, but the traditional choice is barley. Barley malt has a distinctive flavor that is, well, beer-like. Other cereal grains—including wheat, sorghum, corn, and rice—can be used for making beer.. Often, these are used to produce a particular characteristic such as the cloudy lightness of the highly popular summer wheat beers. More often, other grains are used as a cheaper additive for mass-produced beer, to supplement the barley.

Note also that the initial steps in beer production are the same as those for whiskey. However, when making whiskey, the fermented grain beverage is distilled to extract the alcohol, leaving the grain sediment behind.

CHAPTER 1: BEER AND THE DOCTOR

HOPS

Hops are bitter herbs consisting of the female flower clusters of the hop plant. They are such a distinctive part of the flavor of beer that many people cannot imagine beer without hops. Yet, if you consider that beer was being produced and consumed many centuries BCE, then hops are relative newcomers since the first recorded use of hops in beer was in the 11th century in Bavaria.

Prior to that time, many other herbs were used to flavor beer, producing a bitterness to balance the sweetness of the malt. These flavorings included dandelion, heather, horehound, and wormwood, among others. But it was believed that ales made with hops were less prone to spoilage, and hops also added wonderful taste and aroma to beer—so eventually, hops became the additive of choice.

Hops are thought to have antibacterial properties (though I have yet to find a good reference to back this up). Because of this, high levels of hops were added to beer that was destined for long storage. For example, English ales intended to be carried by ship to India received high levels of hops (although the high alcohol content of these beers also retarded spoilage). The resulting India pale ales are very hoppy beers.

Despite the centrality of hops to beer brewing, there are also several types of beers without hops. South African millet beer does not have hops and is not very palatable to Westerners, but I've tasted a number of other beers flavored with spices or fruit. However, though such beverages may be delicious, they do not taste like beer to me.

BEER AND THE DOCTOR

YourBeerNetwork.com (February 2 and 3, 2012)

Alcoholic beverages have been part of human life since the beginning of civilization, when we first learned to cultivate grains. Shortly thereafter, we learned how to ferment grain into alcohol. The art of medicine probably began at the same time, when we learned how to care for the sick, provide comfort, and relieve pain. Alcohol was undoubtedly one of the first medicines. Since that time, the medical arts and alcohol have been linked, if only because they are both integral parts of human existence.

The medical arts and alcohol have been linked in my life, too, as you will see in this collection of vignettes—a semi-autobiographical collection of notes about my life as a doctor. Every doctor has "war stories" about medical school or the early days of residency, and these are some of mine. Beer and other spirits are a common thread in some of the stories—sometimes causative, mostly coincidental—while the other stories are my memories of colorful characters. These stories are all true, though the names have been changed.

BEER, ANYONE?

I grew up in ethnic, Polish Chicago, where beer drinking was a way of life—except in our house. We drank champagne, not just for special occasions, but any time a beer would be called for.

It started with my Uncle Rory. I remember Saturday evenings as a child, when Rory would show up at the house with a couple of six-packs. He and my folks would drink into the night, talking and laughing. Everyone loved Uncle Rory, but it was common knowledge that he drank too much.

One evening he brought a few bottles of cheap champagne. From then on, the Saturday evening parties continued with champagne instead of beer. Years later I asked my father why they switched from beer to champagne. "That's because Rory's doctor said he drank too much beer, and if he didn't stop, it would kill him. So he switched to champagne."

CHAPTER 1: BEER AND THE DOCTOR

A TOUGH PLACE TO STUDY

I studied medicine at Billings Hospital at the University of Chicago, one of the toughest hospitals in Chicago. Now an elite "Center for Advanced Medicine," in the seventies, it served as a community hospital for one of the poorest neighborhoods in the city—and one of the toughest. This was Hyde Park-Kenwood, long before it became gentrified and thus a suitable home for President Obama and his family.

Crime, drugs, alcoholism, and gunshot wounds were common, even among the hospital employees. One week we had more fatal gunshot wounds among the hospital cafeteria workers than in the emergency department. One was a drug-related shooting in the cafeteria, and in the other instance, a jealous husband shot his wife's lover in a drunken rage; both worked in the hospital cafeteria.

After that I brought my lunch from home.

DRINKING WITH MY CADAVER-MATES

I didn't really drink until medical school. Drinking with the other med students is a big part of the bonding experience. Four of us had all been partners on the same cadaver—two on the right side and two on the left—and we would do everything together. In fact, I married my other half on the right side.

Typically, we would join the other med students at Jimmy's (The Woodlawn Tap) to unwind after an exam. But once we went out for a drink *before* an exam. It was the night before Part I of the National Board exams, in our second year of medical school. This was an important test, a make-or-break for doctors.

"Where shall we study for the Boards?" I asked.

Jeffrey, my left cadaver partner, said, "Carol, if we don't know the material by now, we'll never learn it tonight. Let's go for a drink instead."

Who could argue with such logic?

We had a drink at Jimmy's—we were the only med students

there. Then we went to see *The Exorcist,* which had just opened. We all passed our Boards.

TWO GUYS WALK INTO A BAR AND END UP IN THE EMERGENCY ROOM

Medical students who were on their surgical rotations were encouraged to hang around the emergency room to help out and possibly get a chance to practice surgery. Weekends were the best times. One Saturday night, the cops brought in two men with facial cuts they had gotten during a bar fight. They both needed to get stitches, and they were very intoxicated. They were put onto adjacent beds in the emergency ward, separated by privacy curtains—we didn't have individual emergency-room beds in those days.

I helped the surgeon start the stitching, and then he let me take over on my own. Since the patients were on adjacent beds, I was allowed to do both of them. I did a careful job and was very proud of my work, and I threw the curtains back to show it off to the attending surgeon. At that point, the two patients recognized each other—it turns out they had been fighting *each other*! They tried to jump out of bed to continue their fight, and I was caught in the middle.

I learned another lesson that night: it's very easy to subdue belligerent drunks, since they aren't coordinated enough to do any harm. I just used my loudest "mom" voice, scolded them for fighting, and put them back to bed to sleep it off.

DEATH BY AEROSOL

As a medical student, I did a two-week rotation on the inpatient psychiatric ward at Billings Hospital. It was a locked ward. Our job was to look after the physical health of our patients while learning as much as we could about their psychiatric illness.

I was assigned to Frank, a pleasant, fiftysomething man who seemed perfectly normal. Many people with psychiatric illness drink excessively, and Frank was no exception, though he had

CHAPTER 1: BEER AND THE DOCTOR

no trouble stopping when he checked himself into the ward. He was just a regular guy from an ethnic neighborhood in Chicago, a retired factory worker who spent his days at his local bar.

Frank told me there was absolutely nothing wrong with him. He claimed he had no psychiatric problems—he was just hiding out at the hospital so his brother-in-law couldn't find him and kill him. Frank claimed that his brother-in-law had an aerosol can filled with a deadly poison and was following him in close pursuit, trying to spray him to death.

To avoid this, Frank had taken three different buses, in several different directions, running miles on foot between bus stops, until he reached the hospital and voluntarily signed himself into the locked ward for protection. Frank had what is called *delusional disorder, persecutory type*. Except for this one obsession, everything else about his mental state was normal and coherent. He was convinced and convincing.

I was afraid for him to be discharged from the ward—what if he were correct?

EUPHEMISTICALLY SPEAKING

As interns, it was our job to admit patients to the hospital and manage them during their stay. We were on call to take new admissions every third day, and most of our admissions came in from the emergency room, which most local residents used in place of a primary-care physician.

Most patients came in at night, and we'd be up all night to take in new patients, evaluate their medical problems, and start their treatment. In the morning, bright and early, we would go around with the attending physician and the rest of the doctors to see the patients, and the doctors would assist in diagnosis and patient management. The challenge was to discuss the case at the bedside, in front of the patient. We became adept at using Greek and Latin phrases and euphemisms to discuss sensitive medical details in front of a patient. A typical presentation would go like this:

"This 60-year-old man, a known habitual user of two-carbon fragments, presented to the emergency room with *hallucinosis* and *odor spiritus fermentum*. His BAC was .16. He was started on prophylactic diazepam and IV thiamine, to prevent delirium tremens and Korsakoff's. We are monitoring his BAC pending discharge."

The old drunk would lie in bed smiling, enjoying the attention, impressed and pleased that his doctors were discussing him in Latin, totally oblivious to the true meaning of the discussion.

Translation: "This patient, a known alcoholic, showed up in the emergency room seeing pink elephants and smelling of alcohol. He was drunk at twice the legal limit. We gave him Valium to stop the DTs and vitamins to prevent further brain damage. We are letting him sleep it off until his alcohol level drops low enough for discharge."

THE ANIMAL

I was called to the emergency room late one night for my next admission: a big brute of a guy with head trauma who had to be admitted for observation. We interns usually ended up transporting our own patients from the ER to the ward, since the patient-transport service was slow and lazy and patients could die waiting for it (literally).

They handed Tyrone off to me on a gurney. They told me his nickname was "The Animal" and that he was ready to go, except for a small detail—he had to have head x-rays to make sure he didn't have a skull fracture. It appears he had fallen off a second-story balcony but was so drunk that he hadn't felt a thing. Apparently, this was not the first time it had happened.

The emergency room staff was unable to get this burly, muscular, 250-pound man to cooperate for his x-rays, as he tried to hit anyone who came near and he was too heavy to lift. So now, it was my problem.

Fortunately, his wife showed up—all 300 pounds of her. She barged into his room, scolded him for giving the doctors trouble, grabbed him by the ear, and led him to the x-ray machine.

CHAPTER 1: BEER AND THE DOCTOR

Cowed, he followed meekly. Fortunately, his x-rays were normal, and we brought him to his room to sleep it off.

ADDICTS, NEEDLES, AND ANTIBIOTICS

There were many heroin addicts in our neighborhood. Like many of our other patients, they had no regular medical care and used the emergency room as their primary-care physician. Addicts frequently developed serious medical problems as a result of sharing needles. A blood infection that settles on the heart valves, *bacterial endocarditis*, was one of the most dreaded.

This was in the days before AIDS (which later killed many of them). We had a rule: if an IV drug user showed up with a fever that lasted more than a couple of days, we'd admit him or her for observation with the presumption that he or she had bacterial endocarditis. If the diagnosis proved to be correct, then the patient had to stay in the hospital for four to six weeks to get IV antibiotics, two to three times each day. Without this treatment, the patient would die.

To an addict, six weeks in the hospital was like six weeks in jail. He couldn't leave, couldn't do what he wanted—and, worse yet, couldn't smoke, shoot heroin, or drink. Most of our addicts were put on methadone and could sneak out to the yard to catch a smoke, but getting a drink was almost impossible.

For us interns, getting assigned to an IV drug addict for six weeks of antibiotics was no picnic, either. First of all, many of them were in the hospital against their will, and at times, we had to forcibly restrain them (yes, you could get away with it in those days, since we were saving their lives, after all). Worse yet, we had to start IVs in order to treat them.

Back then, all IVs were started by the interns. Typically, most addicts have used up all the "easy" veins for their drug habit, so it could easily take an hour for an intern to find a vein and get an IV line in. I recall one frustrating situation with a 30-year-old addict, Leroy, who had no veins left and didn't particularly want to be in the hospital. I don't know how many times I stuck him with a needle without any success.

Finally, Leroy got sick of being a pincushion. He grabbed the needle from me without a word, put a tourniquet around his leg, and proceeded to put the IV into a small vein between his toes. "There you go, doc. There's your IV in my favorite vein. Now would you please let me get back to sleep?"

I thanked him profusely.

THE BLOOD OF A BRAVE SOLDIER

After I finished my MD, PhD, and oncology training, I joined the faculty at the University of Chicago. I continued my cancer research with a group of scientists who specialized in cancer genetics.

We found a new, rare form of leukemia among blood samples that were sent to the lab for analysis. We tracked it down to a patient in the VA hospital. We needed to get more of his blood cells, hoping to make a breakthrough, and we needed to do it fast, before he died of leukemia. Since I was the most junior member of the lab, they sent me.

Back in those days, we didn't have to go through extensive review panels or get signed consent forms. We just had to ask the patient for a blood sample. So I drove out to the VA hospital, got permission from the ward-attending doctor, and approached the patient. He was pleased to have a visitor, since he clearly loved to talk and had a great sense of humor. He told me he was a veteran of Korea and 'Nam and had been in the hospital for a few weeks already. He didn't mind, though he did miss having his beer on the weekends.

When I asked him for a blood sample for research, he said, "Anything to help leukemia research. But you better get it now, before I croak."

He said he wasn't afraid of dying; he'd seen action on two fronts. He figured he was going to die soon. In fact, he said that his doctor told him not to buy any long-playing records! And his insurance agent sent him a three-month calendar instead of the usual year! So he let me draw his blood, and he gave up six tubes. I thanked him; he laughed. I never saw him again. He died within the week.

CHAPTER 1: BEER AND THE DOCTOR

This veteran's blood did, in fact, help leukemia research, as it helped us to find the mutations that caused his disease. And it launched my own career in medical research, which continued for almost 20 years.

NEW YORK, NEW YORK

During my research years, I took a weekend trip to New York to visit a colleague—a scientist who was on sabbatical leave from London. By then I was single again, and I enjoyed being on my own in New York. I was on the subway on my way to Grand Central Station when the train stopped. An announcement came over the PA system, saying, "This car is out of service because of a medical emergency. Passengers are requested to leave the train and board the express train on the next track."

I ran out and followed two patrolmen to the front car of the subway train to see if I could be of assistance. In the car were a businessman with a suit and a briefcase, the conductor, and the two policemen—all standing over an unkempt old lady slumped over in her seat, looking to be fast asleep. Her hand grasped a dollar bill that someone had probably put in it out of charity.

The businessman spoke. "I think she's dead, but I'm not sure."

"I can tell; I'm a doctor," I volunteered. I reached for her neck to check the carotid pulse, but then I thought twice about reaching for the neck of a possibly armed street person. I checked for a pulse at her wrist, instead.

Her wrist was stone cold. And it was stiff—literally stiff—with rigor mortis. I could have lifted her up by the arm. Likewise, the dollar was wedged tightly in her hand and could not be dislodged, though I'll bet several passengers had tried.

"She's definitely dead," I pronounced.

"Should we call an ambulance?" the cops asked.

"No need to hurry," I said. "She's been dead at least three hours, because that's how long it takes for rigor mortis to set in."

The cops knew her to be an alcoholic, a homeless street lady who panhandled on the subway trains. They took her body to the morgue.

I felt very sad then—sad to realize that a homeless person could die on the subway and ride it to Queens and Manhattan and back for three hours before anyone noticed.

SOUTH AFRICAN WINES

I went to South Africa while I was on sabbatical leave from my university position. This was in 1991, shortly after apartheid had ended and the academic boycott of South African universities had been lifted. My visit to Cape Town was hosted by Professor Patel.

Patel was a South African of Indian background. As a nonwhite, he was fortunate to have a faculty position at the University of Cape Town, one of the few South African universities that remained integrated through apartheid. He took us on a day tour of the Stellenbosch wineries, which are conveniently close to Cape Town. This is South Africa's Napa Valley, producing world-class wines that had been overlooked for years due to trade embargoes.

Patel took us around and had us sample some premier wines. I complimented him on his taste and knowledge of South African wines, saying, "You know these wines so well! You must have been visiting these wineries for years!"

He looked at me with surprise. "Not at all," he said. "Until apartheid was repealed, I would never have been allowed to set foot in a South African winery."

BANTU BEER

During the sabbatical trip, I was treated to a weekend "safari" in Botswana, with a few of the scientists and students from Witwatersrand medical school. To get to Botswana, our group drove north across the Transveld in a couple of VW minibuses. We stopped along the way in a small town for supplies: antimalarial pills, soft drinks, ice, and beer. The town liquor store obliged by providing a few tables and chairs where customers could sit, relax, and drink a cold beer.

CHAPTER 1: BEER AND THE DOCTOR

One of our group suggested I might be interested in a taste of millet beer, a local specialty, so we bought some for me to try. Freshly made and with a short shelf life, it was sold in cartons, like milk. "You can't drink that in here," the proprietor told us, so we left the store and took our purchases along to drink in the vans.

I wondered about the law forbidding drinking millet beer in the store. I learned that, under apartheid, there had been a prohibition on the sale of European liquors to Africans. Millet beer, also known as Bantu beer, was a uniquely African drink, brewed by the indigenous people from millet (a food grain similar to sorghum, which is used in the United States in birdseed). Africans were allowed to buy alcoholic beverages, but they were not allowed to sit in the store and drink. After apartheid was lifted, Africans could purchase anything they liked, but they preferred millet beer because it was familiar and cheaper than anything else. Banning its consumption in the store imposed a de facto continuation of apartheid.

I tried the beer. It was cloudy, like a home brew, and it was very mild, pleasantly carbonated, and bland tasting, with no hop flavor. We continued north, crossing the Limpopo River into Botswana. We had a fun time on our weekend safari, camping out in tents, with a big barbecue around a campfire. The next morning, we took a trip by Land Rover to see the elephants. We were not disappointed. We saw dozens of all sizes and colors—but no pink elephants.

FEELING LUCKY?

Whenever I'd start a month as attending physician on the cancer ward at the university hospital, the previous month's attending would give me charts for all of the patients. (We had paper charts then.) Jim Morgan had been a patient on and off for several months, but he had a very small chart. As it happened, though, most of his medical records were in a much larger chart labeled "Jack Martin."

"Don't worry," I was told, "it's the same man. He had to change his Social Security number and his name because he owed the hospital a lot of money. Not your problem, just take care of his cancer."

Hmmm. Seemed like a good trick that I had not seen before and have not seen since.

Jim was a pleasant fellow, in his forties, much too young to be dying of metastatic prostate cancer. He was surrounded by a crowd of relatives, many of whom moved into his room with him and never left. The family was swarthy, Mediterranean, and spoke a foreign language in addition to English. I asked him what language, and he said, "Romanian." Hmmm.

After reviewing his case, it was clear that he was dying. His cancer had spread everywhere, and the treatment was not working. There was nothing we could do except give him pain medicine. I suggested to him that he stop all the treatment and be discharged, to spend his last few weeks at home, in hospice care. He refused to make a decision until he spoke with his uncle, who was flying in and would be there Saturday. So we waited.

On Saturday morning, the uncle arrived. Or should I say his Godfather? He came by wheelchair, with his entourage. He was an imposing presence and was treated with deference and respect. He listened politely to my evaluation and recommendation, and he thanked me. After I left the room, they conversed for a long time, and then the uncle left. Jim called me in to talk.

"What did you decide?" I asked. Jim's uncle had given him permission to stop treatment, and Jim would be ready to leave in the morning.

"What are you going to do?" I asked.

"First, I'm going to get myself a bottle of red wine and drink it down. Then, I'm going to Vegas," he said. "I'm feeling lucky."

At that moment I realized a few things: (1) Mr. Morgan was anything but lucky. He was dying of prostate cancer at age 43. (2) A number of credit cards, in different aliases, would probably make their way to Las Vegas that week. (3) The "Romani King" is not a legend. He lives, and I've met him.

CHAPTER 1: BEER AND THE DOCTOR

IT'S TIME TO STOP MY CANCER TREATMENT

After 20 years, it was time to leave the university. By then I had remarried, and I wanted to do something different. I gave up cancer research to become a full-time doctor, taking a position as a medical oncologist in a small practice in rural Indiana. No interns, medical students, or research labs—just doctors, nurses, and patients. And the patients were the salt of the earth—for the most part conservative, deeply religious, and living life in moderation.

One of my patients had early-stage breast cancer and was scheduled to come in for chemotherapy every three weeks for a total of eight treatments. Her prognosis was excellent. I saw her in the office just before her second treatment.

"I'm going to stop treatment," she pronounced.

I asked her why. Was it the hair loss? Was she vomiting? Was it that bad?

"No, it wasn't bad at all. But it's ruining my marriage," she said.

I finally got her to explain. It seems that she and her husband were in the habit of having a glass of wine together every evening. One glass. It was their one vice, but the nurses told her she was not allowed to drink while on chemotherapy, so she hadn't had a drink since before the last treatment, three weeks ago. Her husband was getting irritable, and they were beginning to grow apart.

"Just one glass of wine? Of course you can drink a glass of wine daily! It certainly won't hurt you," I said.

"What do I tell the nurses?" she asked.

"Don't tell them if they don't ask. If they do, just say it's the doctor's orders."

She agreed to continue her chemotherapy, and the next time I saw her for chemo, she was beaming. I didn't ask why.

THREE STRIKES AND YOU'RE OUT

Aunty Debby was one of my favorite aunts. Although she was mother to seven of my first cousins, she was not your typical

1950s housewife. Her father, she claimed, had been a bootlegger for Al Capone. During Prohibition she had ridden along with Daddy as a decoy, a little girl covered demurely with a blanket—sitting on a case of whiskey!

Aunty D loved beer, cigarettes, and the Chicago White Sox. In the end, it was the cigarettes that did her in. She had survived two previous early-stage cancers, but when she was diagnosed with cancer for the third time, we knew she would not make it. She had advanced lung cancer.

By then I was an established physician working in another state, but I helped out when I could, answering her questions and providing what support I could.

Aunty D struggled with treatment and said it was the White Sox that kept her going—they had their winningest season ever. She was sure they'd make it this year, after 88 years without a World Series win. Ironically, the Sox did win the 2005 World Series that year. But Aunty Debby died a month before their victory.

A few days after the Series, my cousin picked me up with some White Sox gear to decorate her grave and let her know that her beloved Sox had won. When we arrived, we were surprised to see that every grave in that small cemetery was decorated with White Sox hats and pennants. This was a graveyard filled with loyal Sox fans, who continue to vote Democrat every year!

NELSON MANDELA'S LEGACY

I went back to South Africa years later with my husband, Rick. One of our best memories of the trip was sitting in a sports bar in Cape Town, drinking Tusker beer and watching the crowd as they watched a rugby game on television. The crowd was rowdy, really into the game. Years later, when we saw the movie *Invictus*, we understood the deep-seated rivalry between the South African and New Zealand rugby teams and understood the passion that we had seen in the bar.

During that trip, I was invited to visit the hospital in Baragwanath. I was excited by the chance to visit the cancer

CHAPTER 1: BEER AND THE DOCTOR

ward in this massive hospital of over 3,000 beds. It is one of the biggest hospitals in the world and the only one that served Soweto, the large black township (ghetto) in the suburbs of Johannesburg. Rick was asked what he wanted to do while I was on rounds, and he asked for a tour of Soweto. A few heads were scratched—this was not a typical tour—but they obliged and brought a driver and a tour guide in a minibus.

Apparently, Rick saw every sight in the "little town" of Soweto (population 1.3 million). The visit to Baragwanath hospital was a memorable experience for me, beyond description. At the end of the day, we compared notes. I asked him what was his most memorable experience of the day, and he said, "I visited Nelson Mandela's house, and I peed in his toilet."

RUN FOR CANCER

After many years, I took up running again. It was enjoyable to run along the country roads near home, and it was a good way to let off steam. I ran an occasional 5K race, and I helped to organize our cancer center's annual Run for Research. When my Chicago friend Gary learned that I was running again, he invited me to go on the I Beat Cancer hash in Chicago.

As Gary put it, "I've done hashes for plantar fasciitis, mad cow disease, and swine flu. For what it's worth, it's been five years since my cancer surgery. I've also had plantar fasciitis, but to the best of my knowledge, I've never had mad cow disease or swine flu. The other hashes weren't fund-raisers, and neither is this one. We are not using the words, 'for the cure,' so Susan Komen's people can spend their money on cancer research instead of suing us."

I was intrigued, so I asked, "What's a hash?"

He explained it's a kind of race that starts in a bar and ends in a bar. "Hashers are drinkers with a running problem."

Sadly, I couldn't join the hash because I had to work that day; I was doing my own part to beat cancer. Maybe next year.

GUINNESS POT ROAST

Noreen was a pretty and spirited young woman in her early forties. She was a very Irish lass from South Bend, with dark hair and sparkling eyes. Unfortunately, she was dying of metastatic cancer. We worked hard through the winter, she and I, to get her cancer under control with chemotherapy. We made some progress, but it was a losing fight, and she knew it. She had one request: she wanted to put her treatment on hold for St. Patrick's Day.

"We usually have a big party for St. Pat's. I invite all our friends and acquaintances, and I make my famous *Guinness* pot roast for all," she said.

Her husband raved about the pot roast, so I agreed to wait with treatment for a few weeks, under one condition: she had to give me her recipe for *Guinness* pot roast. We had a deal.

I saw her later in March, and we started treatment again. But eventually, she succumbed. I tried the pot roast recipe after I heard about her death. She was right; it was excellent. I still think of her every St. Patrick's Day, and I still make the pot roast. (See chapter 7 for the recipe.)

SPRING PEEPERS

It was Friday, the end of an especially difficult week. We had lost a few cancer patients, and everyone in the clinic was a bit down. It was cold and dark at the end of February, and it seemed like winter would never end.

In the evening, Rick picked me up to drive us to our house in the Dunes. As we drove through the wetlands, he stopped and opened the windows. I could hear them, the spring peepers. In the early spring, these frogs are the first to awaken, and they start their plaintive calls when the rest of the world is still silent. You could hear each individual frog's call, and they sounded like lost souls. To me, they were the first sign of a coming spring—a sign that things were starting to get better.

Rick rolled up the windows, saying, "Come on. Let's go. You need a beer."

CHAPTER 1: BEER AND THE DOCTOR

MENTORING MEDICAL STUDENTS IN THE BEER CLINIC

YourBeerNetwork.com (March 26, 2011)

A few months ago, I was visiting one of my favorite beer bars, the Map Room in Chicago. This is a classy joint that has a national reputation as a great place to enjoy many different types of beer, draft (26 taps) or bottles (over 200 brands). In other words, it's my kind of place.

Because of the selection and quality, the drinks are a bit pricier than they are at your usual *Bud Light* bar, so the Map Room attracts an upscale clientele who can afford to drink there: boomers with money (me), young professionals with downtown jobs, and students in professional school. (You have to take out really big loans to go to law school or med school, so as a result, you have extra spending money.)

I was enjoying a Belgian draft and scrutinizing the beer list for my next pick when a young woman sat at the empty stool next to me. She looked perplexed. She turned to me and said, "You seem to be enjoying your beer. Can you suggest something for me?"

She admitted she really didn't drink much beer but wanted to give it a try and didn't know where to start. I asked about her preferences (which ran toward highly sweetened cocktails) and picked out a few "easy" beers. I suggested we ask the bartender for a taste of each.

"You mean they let you do that?" she asked, naively. I explained why it was OK to ask the bartender for a taste of his drafts—he appreciates your interest, and he sells more beer that way. As I expected, she really liked the *Duchesse de Bourgogne*, a refreshing Flemish red ale that tastes a lot like cherry soda, though it contains no fruit. It is a good introduction to the Belgian ale genre.

TO YOUR HEALTH!

While she was tasting her draft, I took a wild guess and asked her if she was a student.

"Yes, "she said, "I'm a medical student."

"Where?" I asked.

"University of Chicago, Pritzker School," she answered brightly.

"What a coincidence!" I said. "I went to med school there, too, and I also taught on the faculty for years."

"No kidding!" she said. "My parents went there, too! What year did you graduate?"

I told her and she said, "Omigod, my folks graduated the same year!"

Gulp.... Yes, I remembered Larry and Karen (not their real names). I hadn't seen them since graduation. We caught up on news and exchanged contact info. She thanked me for introducing her to Belgian beers and then ... paid my tab! Boy, did I feel old! Her folks had moved on to career and family and were ready to retire ... and I was still practicing medicine and drinking beer in bars!

As you've read, I started drinking beer in medical school. Med school is a lot like summer camp—there are many group activities (exams, parties, team sports, and dissecting cadavers), and going to a bar with other med students is a good way to bond, as well as to let off steam. Beer is the quintessential social beverage. You can't drink beer alone.

Try it. Go into a bar and sit by yourself and order a whiskey. No one will bother you. Now order a beer. Pretty soon someone will sit next to you and start chatting with you, and the bartender will join in, and a med student will walk up and ask your opinion.

Even if you enjoy a cold longneck at home at the end of your workday, you will not be drinking alone because you will be turning on the TV to see your favorite sports team or your TV sitcom friends (reruns of *Cheers?*).

My theory is that the taste of a specific beer evokes a memory of a person or event that will forever come to mind when you drink the beer again—not unlike Proust's remembrances of childhood evoked by smells. Perhaps that's one of the yet undis-

CHAPTER 1: BEER AND THE DOCTOR

Rick, enjoying a Leffe Blonde *on draft at Au Dernier Metro bar, Paris.*

Dr. Westbrook, ready for oncology clinic in Goshen, Indiana, 2008.

covered characteristics of hops. And that is part of the process of beer appreciation—you begin to remember the taste of a beer as you associate it with a specific social event or person, and as you "acquire" more beers, you have a wider social context and become a member of the community of beer aficionados.

Although I drank beer in med school, I didn't appreciate it much. Back then we didn't have much selection besides the beers from Budweiser, Miller, and Schlitz. As a matter of fact, our group preferred single-malt scotch to beer since it had more character compared to the beers of the 1970s. It wasn't until I went to England and discovered real ales on draft—and real pubs—that I developed a taste for beer.

In England we discovered Theakston's *Old Peculier* at the Grange Bar in the London Borough of Ealing. What a fabulous, dark, malty, high-alcohol ale! Tasting it now brings back memories of good times in the United Kingdom. We spent months trying to find it in Chicago (in bottles) and discovered Delilah's Bar, with its funky draft beers and "punk music nights" on Mondays.

We learned to drink Belgian beers in Paris—I remember one late night sitting in a bar drinking *Leffe Blonde* and having a "conversation" with a young Basque soldier, even though we didn't have a common language. And to this day, the taste of *Harpoon IPA* reminds me of consuming large bowls of steamed clams with my husband at the Union Oyster House in Boston, shortly after we moved there. And I'm sure you have stories of your own for each beer that you like!

I have a feeling that my young medical student will always remember her experience with the *Duchesse* at the Map Room. I predict that she will move on to more challenging and even better beers and will soon be an expert on the subject, like her mentor (me). And the more you learn, the more you appreciate a good beer.

So here are some lessons from *The Beer Clinic* on how to appreciate beer:

1. First, you have to *drink* it. Find yourself a beer bar that has a good selection, preferably on draft—and by all means, ask your bartender for tastes.

CHAPTER 1: BEER AND THE DOCTOR

2. Drink only good beer! That means no mass-produced lagers. No *Bud, Bud Light, Coors*, etc. If they don't have any craft beer available, then drink a gin and tonic or rum and Coke® instead.

3. Taste all the different styles of beer and learn to tell them apart. One of the nice things about being a beer aficionado is that it's a lot easier than becoming a wine expert. For one thing, there is a limited number of beer styles, so you can get to know them all.

4. Find a style that you like and concentrate on that for a while, to the exclusion of everything else, as you try different breweries' versions. During our *Old Peculier* phase, we drank only dark ales and porters.

5. Start simple and light—with pilsners and cream stouts—and move on to stronger-tasting beers, such as American IPAs or the complex Belgian abbey ales.

6. Pick out a few good regional beers that are available in bottles so you will always have something to order at a bar if there is nothing appealing on draft.

7. When you are uncertain what to drink in a strange bar, you can't go wrong if you stick to the draft list and select local or regional microbrews—usually, they are the freshest kegs on the bar.

8. Finally, cultivate good social experiences while you drink your beer. Not only will this help you remember your newfound beers, but you will have a good time doing it.

CHAPTER 2

THE BASICS: LESSONS IN BEER STYLES AND INGREDIENTS

From its inception, YourBeerNetwork.com was meant for the sophisticated beer drinker. Our purpose was not to educate the beer novice but to enrich the drinking experience of those who knew and loved craft beer.

As a staff writer, I had two areas of expertise to contribute. First, I was a doctor, so I could speak authoritatively about the biochemical and medicinal implications of beer. Second, I was a home brewer, which gave me practical knowledge of hops, barley, and yeast. I shared some of this home-brewing knowledge with my editor, Harvey Gold, at our first meeting—which became the start of a lasting friendship (see "The Beer Doctor Makes a House Call," below).

Later, I learned even more about hops in preparation for making a home brew; I write about this in "The Hops Project," below. The remaining articles form a three-part "course" that covers the basics of craft beer; they were written at the request of many friends who were new to the craft beer scene and wanted to learn more about it.

Too basic for YourBeerNetwork.com's readership, the *Beer Clinic* lessons on craft beer were published in our local community newsletter, *Sand Tracks*, and in the national blog *3QuarksDaily.com*. I hope the beginning beer drinker will find these lessons a helpful and entertaining introduction to the world of craft beer.

CHAPTER 2: THE BASICS

THE BEER DOCTOR MAKES A HOUSE CALL

YourBeerNetwork.com (March 13, 2011)

It was late February, and I was on a road trip to visit my friends in Youngstown. Since Akron is directly on the way to Youngstown, I had no excuse. It was time to finally meet my editor, with whom I previously had had only a virtual acquaintance.

Because Harvey was making such good progress in his appreciation of beer, I realized he was ready for an advanced beer class. It was time for Beer 201: The Flavors of Beer. I brought along some beer-making ingredients and a few bottles of my home brew.

I was greeted by Harvey and his wife, Dolli, and we were friends immediately. The Golds live in a converted old schoolhouse, filled with unusual antiques and unique artifacts from around the world. It's a perfect place for a lesson on the unique flavors of the world's beers.

[Note: if you would like to follow along with the lesson and experience these tastes, you can purchase all the necessary ingredients for under $20 from an online home-brewer supplier—such as MidwestSupplies.com, RebelBrewer.com, or GrapeandGranary.com.]

We started class with the most subtle of beer flavors—the malts. To beer, malts are the bread on which you spread your butter (hops). The taste is subtle but unmistakable. We tasted six varieties of dried malted barley. Dried malted barley looks a lot like grass seed, only a bit plumper. Chew on a few grains and . . . surprise! You expect a bland, raw cereal taste, but instead, you find that the malted barley is extremely sweet and crunchy, like honey granola. That's because the bland grain starches in barley are converted into sweet sugar—maltose—when the grain is sprouted (malted). The sprouted grain is then dried and made ready to use for brewing. The sugars are all used up in the brewing process, but the bread/grain flavor remains.

We tasted our first malt, and Harvey exclaimed, "Why, that tastes like a Dunkel!" And he was correct. This was Munich malt, a common ingredient of German beers, including bocks and Oktoberfest beers. It is lightly kiln dried, giving a slight toasted flavor and imparting a dark gold color to the beer.

Gambrinus honey malt was next. This is a light, untoasted malt. It has an exquisitely sweet honey flavor and is very smooth. Next, two Belgians: Belgian biscuit malt is used in European beers and imparts a bread-like taste and a red-brown color, while Belgian aromatic malt has solid malt flavor and a strong malt aroma.

Finally, we tasted two dark malts, which are heavily kiln roasted to a dark brown or espresso black. These two dark roasts are called chocolate malt and black patent malt, respectively. Dark malts contain little or no residual sugar, so they are used for flavoring and color, not for fermentation. You can taste them in stouts and porters. And yes, chocolate malt does have a faint chocolate taste.

Next lesson: hops. When people say they don't like beer, they usually mean they don't like the flavor of strong hops. Hops can be very bitter and overpowering—but there are also mild varieties with exquisite flavor and everything in between. Hops are the dried, fragrant flowers of the hop plant. For the home brewer, these are available in compressed pellets, which are added to the brew pot as needed.

I brought a selection of hops to taste, or rather, to smell. We began with Cascade and Centennial hops. One whiff and you immediately recognize the taste of an American IPA. Cascade and its brother Centennial were developed in the United States and represent the predominant—and I would say overused—flavors in most American-style ales. The taste is described as floral, spicy, and citrusy.

At the opposite end of the spectrum are Fuggles and Kent Goldings, used in mild English bitters. Dolli described the flavor as that of fresh-cut grass, and she was correct. The descriptions are mild, grassy, and woody (Fuggles) or pleasant, soft, and earthy (Kent Goldings).

CHAPTER 2: THE BASICS

Without going into detail about alpha and beta hop acids, suffice it to say that some of these hops are used for bittering, some for flavoring, and some strictly for aroma. Liberty is an aroma hop developed in the United States as a substitute for the classic German hop, Hallertauer Mittelfrüh—probably because it is easier to pronounce. It has a mild but lingering aroma.

Other flavors are used in beer, but almost always in addition to hops. Coriander is a frequent addition to Belgian beers, as is orange peel, which we sampled in this lesson. Other flavors include fruit (used in Belgian lambics), sweet spice (in Christmas ale and pumpkin ale), coffee (in coffee ale), and lactose or milk sugar (in milk stout). Chocolate is used sparingly, if at all, in chocolate stouts and porters; these brews get most of their flavor from darker, aromatic malts that impart a dark brown color and a sweet taste reminiscent of chocolate.

What do yeasts eat? Sugars. We tasted dried malt extract—DME—a brewing ingredient extracted from malts and added directly to the brew pot. It is a pale yellow powder, intensely sweet and reminiscent of the centers of malted milk balls (which is precisely what it is). Belgian candi sugar, also used for brewing, is crystallized pure beet sugar (table sugar) in the form of rock candy. Like a lot of adults, yeasts can't digest lactose (meaning milk sugar), so lactose can be used as a sweetener without increasing the alcohol content.

What can you say about yeasts? There is an endless variety of strains that produce everything from beer and wine to cider, whiskey, vinegar, bread, cheese, and penicillin. There are hundreds of yeast strains for beer brewing alone! Yeasts break down the basic components of the brew mash and convert them to alcohol and carbon dioxide, but they also produce a small amount of complex molecular compounds. These trace compounds impart distinctive flavors that are hard to describe and cannot be tasted directly.

The best way to appreciate the yeast in a beer is to taste it. I focused on Belgian yeasts, which produce a distinctive, almost medicinal flavor. Belgian beers are an acquired taste—and they are too easily acquired and frequently addictive.

I brought two home brews made with Belgian yeasts. One, a light abbey ale similar to *Leffe*, was made with biscuit malts and lightly hopped with Styrian Golding hops. But it has a strong flavor from the yeast, a Wyeast Belgian Abbey II #1762. Compare the taste to that of a mild beer, such as an English bitter or a light lager, and you can spot the flavor immediately.

The other home brew I brought was a "clone" (copy) of *Tripel Karmeliet* (also a Belgian), brewed with light malts and hops and Wyeast Belgian Abbey #1214. The beer is spiced with coriander, but you can taste the Belgian yeast flavor as well.

We ended our lesson with a visit to the Golds' favorite local diner, where we had huge salads and the best Reuben sandwich west of New York. I would have paired these strong flavors with a strong Belgian or a barley wine, but alas, I was on a road trip. No beer for the Beer Doctor, this time.

THE HOPS PROJECT: A RESEARCH PROJECT INTO THE CHEMISTRY, BIOCHEMISTRY, AND FLAVOR OF BEER

YourBeerNetwork.com (April 29, 2014)

The hops project began at Christmas 2013, when I was given a one-pound bag of Cascade hop pellets, ready for brewing. The hops were harvested in the fall of 2013 at my son's in-laws' Empire Hops Farm in Michigan (http://empirehopsfarm.com).

One pound is a lot of hops for a home brewer, enough to make 16 five-gallon batches of IPA! I could never hope to give away 80 gallons of beer in a year, much less consume it. My solution: put more hops in each batch of beer.

I wasn't sure my standard IPA recipe would hold up to five times more hops, and I would almost certainly have to increase the malt and alcohol content of the beer; in other words, I would

CHAPTER 2: THE BASICS

probably have to create a new recipe for an ultrahopped IPA. So I realized that, before going ahead with this challenge, I needed to learn more about hops.

Thus, the hops project began. I approached this like a laboratory research project: first, I did the background research into the biochemistry of hops; next, I asked the experts for advice; and finally, I did the fieldwork—creating my brew and comparing it to a variety of hoppy ales.

In part 1, we'll cover the science; in part 2, we'll discuss the hops, which, as you know, are the flowers of the hop vine—*Humulus lupulus*, to be exact. They contain a variety of compounds that add bitterness, flavor, and aroma to the beer. The main flavor comes from alpha acids, beta acids, and volatile oils.

THE BIOCHEMISTRY OF HOPS

Fresh or dried hops are added to the boiling wort (a liquid made of malt, sugar, and water) prior to fermentation, to add bitterness and flavor to the beer. Hops can also be added after fermentation is complete and can be allowed to steep for a few days, almost like a tea bag. This process, called *dry hopping*, adds hop aroma but little flavor.

The chemistry of these processes is fairly well understood nowadays. Hops contain a mixture of "alpha acids," of which the main compound is *humulone*. Humulone is not very soluble, but prolonged boiling converts it into *isohumulone*, which is very water soluble.

Hops producers give the percentage of total alpha acid units by weight (AAU); they're an indication of how much bitterness can theoretically be extracted during brewing. Alpha acids are the main flavor component of American hops, such as Cascade, Centennial, Willamette, Citra, Simcoe, etc. American hops are the major taste components in IPAs and American ales, and their flavors are described as citrus, grapefruit, piney, or fruity. Home brewers make use of the AAU percentage to estimate the level of bitterness (hoppiness) their brew will achieve.

Hops also contain *beta acids*. Beta acids do not require boiling but develop their bitter flavor by oxidation during fermentation and storage. They are an important component of noble hops, which are Hallertau, Spalt, Tettnang, and Czech Saaz. You will recognize them as the main flavors of German lagers, providing a smooth bitterness and spicy, peppery, or floral taste. American home brewers generally don't take into consideration the beta acid content of their hops (which is generally not provided by retail hops suppliers), but beta acid content is important to commercial brewers.

Other important components of hops are the essential oils, of which one of the most important is *humulene*. Humulene is thought to give the "noble" character to noble hops. These essential oils are quite volatile, so they are driven off by boiling. Because of this volatility, you can smell them more easily than you can taste them, and they are put into a beer by dry hopping.

Essential oils are important flavor elements in English hops (Fuggles, East Kent Goldings, etc.), which are otherwise low in alpha hops. English hops are described as herbal, grassy, earthy, or fruity. Many American hops also contain high levels of essential oils and can be used for dry hopping as well as for bittering (boiling).

And then there is…everything else. Sometimes, it's the minor aromatics and chemicals present in small amounts that provide the distinctive flavor to other hop varieties. A good brewer or beer drinker can taste the differences.

Prior to tasting a new beer, I want to know how hoppy I can expect it to be. A measure of the hoppiness (also called bitterness) is provided by the IBU, or International Bittering Unit. In a commercial brewery, the IBU is determined by chemical analysis, using a spectrophotometer to measure the total content of alpha acids. We home brewers don't have access to spectrophotometers, so we generally calculate an approximate IBU based on the AAUs of the hops that we add, plus a few other fudge factors.

For example, my Cascade hops were labeled as having 9.3% AAU (alpha acid units). If I used four times the amount of hops from my usual brew, my calculations suggested I would achieve

CHAPTER 2: THE BASICS

166 IBU. This would need more malt and higher alcohol—making it a double IPA.

ASKING THE EXPERTS

At this point, I had enough background information to ask a few brewing experts for some direction before proceeding on my own. I decided to go for it.

I got in touch with Jaime Jurado, a good friend who happens to be the director of brewing operations at Abita Brewing Company. I asked him, "How hoppy can you make a beer? What about these beers that advertise IBUs in the 500s or higher—are those numbers accurate? Is there a limit to the solubility of the hop oils? Can you even taste the hops at high IBU? Do you need to add more malt and a higher alcohol level to make a hoppy beer taste palatable?"

He replied, "I don't know if 2500 IBU is physically attainable. The higher the IBU, the more unreliable the analysis. What we do know is that there is a maximum hop intensity that our palates can detect and discern. My opinion is that balance is always important, so more malt backbone helps balance very hoppy beers—hence, the double and tripel IPAs out there. But if you ask 10 brewmasters, you'll certainly receive 14 opinions—maybe more."

Jaime referred me to a brewer friend of his, Karl Ockert, the technical director for the MBAA (Master Brewers Association of the Americas). Karl got back to me with the following:

> The maximum solubility of the iso-alpha acids is about 120 ppm, which means, theoretically, the maximum IBU possible is about 155. Sensory-wise, you probably could not detect any real difference in IBUs above 80 anyway.
>
> To make any beer palatable at the high end of the IBU range requires a significant alcohol and dextrin content; hence, you see 100 IBU double and tripel IPAs at 6–10% ABV. Ironically, the higher the gravity of the

wort to make the beer [i.e., the higher the malt and alcohol content], the less efficient the isomerization and solubility of the alpha acid. In other words, the stronger the beer, the less easy it is to make it super bitter.

The analysis loses accuracy at higher IBU levels, and the breweries representing numbers above 100–120 are probably using dodgy methods of analysis or relying upon calculated values that ignore the limiting solubility factors.

In other words, there aren't any rules, but it's a matter of taste, and most tasters find that higher hops are balanced with more malt and higher alcohol.

MY HOME BREW

Armed with this information and encouragement, it was time to design my hoppy IPA. I decided to modify my standard 6.5% IPA recipe, using three additions of Cascade hops over 90 minutes, a fourth at the end of the boil, and a dry hop as well. I would balance the flavor by increasing the dried malt extract by 30% and add some extra mouthfeel to the whole grain "mini-mash" with biscuit malt, which has a bread-like flavor.

Three additions of hops during the boil, plus a fourth during the last 10 minutes, would give me an IBU of about 124. The ABV would be about 7.5%. This was my *90-Minute Empire IPA*, a single-hop double IPA named for the Michigan hop farm.

I brewed the beer, and it was ready by Super Bowl Sunday, which provided the perfect time to taste it and compare it to a variety of commercially produced high-IBU beers. I wanted to see if alcohol and malt had an impact on the flavor and how other high-IBU beers compared to my brew.

I picked up seven hoppy craft beers, listed in order from lowest to highest (below), and threw in a rye IPA to see if the grain type made a difference. (These estimates of IBUs may not be accurate; I found them on a variety of websites, so take them with a grain of salt.) I tasted all the beers during the first quarter of the

CHAPTER 2: THE BASICS

game, accompanied by the requisite wings and chips, with assistance from my husband, Rick. We started with the lower IBUs and worked our way up to the highest. Here is the list:

Table 1: IBU and % ABV of Hoppy Craft Beers

	IBU	ABV
Victory *HopDevil*	50	6.7%
Sierra Nevada *Celebration*	65	6.8%
Sierra Nevada *Torpedo*	70	7.2%
Anderson *Hop Ottin IPA*	78	7.0%
Dogfish Head *90 Minute IPA*	90	9.0%
Southern Tier *2X IPA*	90	8.2%
Six Point *Resin Imperial IPA*	103	9.1%
Star Hill *Double Platinum*	180	8.5%

Compared to:

Southern Tier *2X Rye IPA*	50-60	8.1%
Westbrook's *90 Minute Empire IPA*	124	7.8%

I do not have the space to review these beers individually. Suffice it to say they were all world-class; which you prefer is simply a matter of personal taste. The first two beers were typical, big-flavored American IPAs, with *Celebration* boasting the use of fresh hops. The fresh hops add an herbal or grassy flavor that is mellow and pleasant.

As our tasting proceeded up the IBU ladder, the increasing bitterness was apparent. Note that the next two, *Torpedo* and *Hop Ottin*, had more hop bitterness than *Celebration* and *HopDevil* but about the same degree of malt and alcohol (low 70s). I thought the hops were a bit harsh-tasting in *Torpedo* and *Hop Ottin*, confirming my suspicion that higher malt and alcohol levels were a necessary complement to the taste of hops.

The next beers on the list, Southern Tier *2X IPA* and Dogfish Head *90 Minute IPA*, had a much better balance between hops, malt, and alcohol. In this middle range, Dogfish Head *90 Minute IPA* clearly stood out as a world-class beer. However, Southern

Tier *2X IPA* came in a close second—also well-balanced and very drinkable.

Interestingly, to my palate, the hops in Southern Tier *2X IPA* tasted almost exactly the same as those in its less hoppy cousin, Southern Tier *2X Rye IPA*. I might conclude that barley malt moderates the hop taste better than does rye malt.

The hoppiest-tasting beer was *Resin*, from Six Point—it was quite an experience to drink this beer, which stood head and shoulders above the others in extreme hoppy taste. The high alcohol gave it an extra kick. Interestingly, *Double Platinum* claims an IBU of 180, and it was certainly hoppy, but not nearly as much (to my palate) as *Resin Imperial IPA*. Was it a trick of good malt and alcohol balance that made *Resin* taste stronger, or were the measurements inaccurate? I liked both beers, but they were surprisingly different.

How did my home brew, Westbrook's *90-Minute Empire IPA*, stack up? It was a damn good beer. Surprisingly, though, it did not taste as if it contained 124 IBUs, like *Resin* does, but rather, it landed in the middle. In malt taste and hop flavor, it seemed very close to the Southern Tier *2X IPA*. I would guess it was about 90 IBUs.

So my hops and malt were perfectly balanced, but my IBU calculation was a bit off, or my hops extraction was not as efficient as I had hoped. Either way, my home brew was a very good beer indeed, perfect for the Super Bowl. It paired well with our hot wings and spicy chili.

CRAFT BEER 101: WHAT IS THE "CRAFT" IN "CRAFT BEER"?

Sand Tracks, Beverly Shores, Indiana, Spring 2013

If your idea of the perfect beer is a *Bud*, swigged down while watching the game, read no further... this section is NOT for

CHAPTER 2: THE BASICS

you. But if you are a food snob, a gourmand, a connoisseur of fine wines and spirits, or merely hop-curious, then read on.

Craft beer is the latest craze among foodies. What's the hype all about? And how do you get on the bandwagon? In the next few sections, we'll tell you everything you need to know about craft beer and teach you how to enjoy it, in three easy lessons.

First of all, what is craft beer? Craft beer is defined by what it is NOT. It is not mass-produced out of cheap ingredients, widely distributed (inter)nationally, or tasteless—for the most part. It is not brewed in large batches (only small ones), and it is not distributed nationally (only regionally). And it does not taste like *Budweiser*!

Craft beers have unique flavors, rich and complex. Craft beer is not *made*—it is *crafted* by a brewmaster using quality ingredients. And you need to know about the ingredients if you want to become a craft beer snob.

The main ingredients in craft beer are hops and barley. Barley, a grain, is sprouted (malted), which converts the bland starch into sugar—the same sweet malt found inside malted milk balls and chocolate malt shakes! Yeast converts the malt sugar into alcohol and carbon dioxide gas—the bubbles that create the beer foam.

After the fermentable sugar is used up by the yeast, what remains are other carbohydrates and malt proteins that provide a distinctive bread-like flavor, providing body and character. The more malt that is fermented, the higher the resulting alcohol and the more flavorful the beer. You can raise the alcohol content of beer by using other, less expensive sugars, but they add no malt flavor.

Malted barley produces more sugar than do most other grains, and its enzymes can malt other grains as well; furthermore, barley grows abundantly in northern climates that cannot sustain wine grapes. It's not surprising, then, that beer made from barley became the fermented beverage of choice in northern Europe.

The hop is the flower of the hop vine, and this herb has been used since the Middle Ages to flavor beer. Unlike other flavoring spices, hops grow well in the colder climates where barley is grown. Hops inhibit the growth of bacteria, but not of yeast, so they help prevent beer spoilage. High amounts of hops were added to help preserve beer in kegs that were going to be shipped to India, a journey that took many months—giving rise to the India pale ale, or IPA, beer style. Like many adult foods (e.g., caviar, green olives), hops are an acquired taste, but once you cultivate a taste for hops, you will seek them out.

Finally, the yeast. This microbe defines the beer *style*. There are two main types of yeast, the top-fermenting and the bottom-fermenting—giving rise to the two major beer styles, the ale and the lager, respectively. These two brewing styles developed independently in European countries: lagers in the colder, northern climates, and ales in the more temperate climates of Belgium and England, as the two yeasts work best at 50 and 70 degrees, respectively.

Although brewing lagers takes longer at low temperatures, a process known as *continuous fermentation* was developed in 1953. It enables rapid brewing of lagers with cheaper ingredients and less flavor. Thus, it became possible to mass-produce lager beers by replacing some malt with cheaper grain; for example, Budweiser contains 30% rice, only 4.5% alcohol, and minimal hop character.

These light lagers, which have come to dominate the world market, are the antithesis of craft beers. Cheaper to produce and sell than well-crafted beers, light lagers are responsible for the loss of many regional breweries and the decline of American brewing, which is only now being revived by the craft beer movement.

The flavor palette available with malt, hops, and yeast is extensive. To this variety, add the variation in alcohol content, the use of other grains such as wheat or oats, and the addition of minor flavors (e.g., spice, fruit)—and the combinations are limitless. Putting these ingredients together to brew a beverage that is beautiful to look at, delightful to taste, and refreshing to drink—that is the craft in craft beer.

CHAPTER 2: THE BASICS

BASIC BEER STYLES

The number of different beers can be overwhelming. Where does the novice begin? First, it helps to understand a few of the basic beer styles. Then, you should taste a variety of beers to see which ones you prefer, developing your own palate. Finally, based on your experience, you'll be able to read a beer list and select those that suit your tastes.

As you try more beers, you will develop an appreciation of the finer points of hops and barley. In our first assignment, we will taste the basic beer styles and learn to appreciate the malt, hops, and yeast flavors in each.

Assignment 1: Distinguish the two main beer styles and understand the contribution of barley and hops.

In this assignment, we will taste and compare a few bottles of beer. You may need to go to a beer store to find the craft beers; your local supermarket probably carries only mass-market beer (assuming you live in a state where supermarkets are allowed to sell beer).

1. First, we will compare a mass-produced lager to its prototype, a good German or Czech lager. Get yourself a *Bud* (the last one you will ever drink) and a bottle of good German lager. I suggest *Warsteiner Premium Verum*, *Bitburger Premium Pils*, or *Pilsner Urquell*. Pour the *Bud* and the German beer into adjacent glasses. Note the color, head, and aroma of each. Then sip the German beer. Love that pilsner malt and those mild hops. Now taste the *Budweiser*. Soda pop carbonation, watery, and almost flavorless, with a bitter aftertaste. Are you a convert?

2. Next, for the ale and the hop flavor, we will start with an American Pale Ale. This is the most popular ale style in the United States. It is light and relatively low in alcohol (4.5–5% ABV), with a distinctive American hop flavor. One of the most popular and readily available is *Sierra Nevada Pale Ale*. With a nice color and a good head, this

beer has a mild hop palate, but its palate is much more pronounced than the German lager's. *Sierra Nevada* is hopped with American Cascade hops and Magnum hops, which give it a citrusy and pleasantly pungent flavor.

Assignment 2: Abide by the *Beer Clinic* rules:

1. Give up mass-market lagers. These include "pretend" craft beers, which are merely flavored, mass-market lagers (for example, *Shock Top*), and "export" lager beers, which are the same as *Bud* but made in another country (*Corona, Red Stripe, Fosters*, etc.)

2. Until you have mastered hops and malts, do not drink beers that have been flavored to disguise their basic beer tastes, such as pumpkin ales, Christmas ales, vanilla porters, and fruit beers.

3. Never drink beer from a bottle. Use a glass to fully appreciate the color, aroma, mouthfeel, and head. Use a pint glass for ales and lagers and a goblet for the higher-alcohol and aromatic beers.

CRAFT BEER 102: BEERS OF THE WORLD—DEVELOPING YOUR BEER PALATE

Sand Tracks, Beverly Shores, Indiana, Spring 2013

Welcome back to *The Beer Clinic!* In Craft Beer 101, we learned the basics of craft beer and introduced the two main brewing styles: the lager and the ale. Here in Craft Beer 102, we'll go over the beers that have evolved from these styles around the world. In today's class assignment, you will taste them all and begin to develop your own preferences.

CHAPTER 2: THE BASICS

At first it seems overwhelming—the possible combinations of malts, hops, and yeast must result in thousands of beers. Yet the number of beer styles is really quite small—even fewer than wine styles. That's because each beer evolved in a geographic area with a limited selection of local ingredients. With trial and error, the best tasting of these beers gained popularity, and the unpalatable combinations were discarded.

These basic beer styles have stood the test of time, and many are still produced in their place of origin using local ingredients, continuing the tradition over hundreds of years. Each has its own interesting history, which is fun to learn, as it adds character and pleasure to the tasting experience. To fully appreciate these beers, you have to *taste* them, not merely read about them. This is the first step in understanding what makes a good beer and what craft brewers are trying to emulate or surpass.

If you want to drink the beer at its best—on draft—you'll need to find a venue that serves draft beer. There is no substitute for a trip to Munich to drink Oktoberfest beers or a rowdy evening in an Irish pub drinking *Guinness*. Sadly, the availability of draft imports is limited, unless you travel to a specialty beer bar.

Fortunately, many good world beers are available in bottles. Don't look in supermarkets, which carry only mass-market lagers; instead, purchase world beers in a good liquor store. You may find a salesperson who knows something about beer. Remember, many beers are made and distributed in small batches and are not always on the shelf when you want them. (Tip: check the expiration date before you buy any beer, especially imports.)

Following is a list of the beer styles of the world and a recommendation for tasting each. Your assignment is as follows:

1. Taste one beer from each category. Keep a checklist, and include your own ratings.

2. Choose a style you like and then seek out craft beers of the same style from regional breweries, preferably on draft. Compare to the original, take notes on your preferences, and develop your palate for this style.

Follow these steps: Never drink from a bottle. Pour the beer into a glass. Look at the color and clarity and enjoy the aroma. Taste the foamy head, an oft-overlooked pleasure. Finally, sip the beer and then drink up.

Pay attention to the alcohol content, or percentage of alcohol by volume (% ABV), because you might inadvertently overdo it, especially if you are used to lite beer. Two 7% ABV beers in a standard 16-ounce draft mug is the equivalent of four 12-ounce bottles of *Budweiser* (4.5% ABV).

For part 2 of this assignment, you will need to find craft beers, either in bottles or on draft. Find a restaurant that serves craft beer, or find a good beer bar. Skip bars that serve only mass-market lagers. Brewpubs are great venues for tasting beer styles, but their draft list is limited to what they produce, so you won't get an all-around experience for this lesson. But a field trip to a good brewery tasting room—for example, Bell's in Kalamazoo, Michigan—is an unforgettable experience.

Following are examples of a variety of world craft beers:

1. **German-style lagers:** *Warsteiner Premium Verum, Bitburger Premium Pils,* and *Pilsner Urquell*

    We noted in Beer 101 that the above lagers fall into this category. Variations include pilsners and kölsch. Lagers go well with bratwurst, picnic foods, salty foods, and pretzels, and they're great for breakfast.

2. **Bock or dubbelbock:** *Paulaner Salvator, Hofbräu Maibock*

    A bock beer is a lager that is made with more malt and less hop flavor. The result is a sweeter beer with a lovely off-white head and a higher alcohol content, usually in the range of 6 to 7% ABV. A dubbelbock uses double the malt, with alcohol content up to 12% ABV. Bocks were first brewed by the Paulist monks in 17th-century Munich for Lenten consumption, as their rigorous

CHAPTER 2: THE BASICS

diet permitted no solid food from Ash Wednesday to Easter. A solid beer diet for 40 days brought them closer to heaven. Bocks go well with hearty food, stews, or roasts—or with nothing, during Lent.

3. **Wheat beers:** *Franziskaner Hefe-Weisse,* Hacker-Pschorr *Weisse, Blanche de Bruxelles*

   Wheat beers are light, refreshing beverages made with 50 percent or more wheat grain. They are light colored and cloudy (unfiltered), with a spicy flavor that comes from botanicals (coriander or orange peel). The yeast itself may provide a fruity taste. The American adaptation of this beer adds extra sugar or fruit juice. Best in the summer, wheat beers go with salads, light food, fruit, ice cream, or Jell-O.

4. **English bitters:** *Wells Bombardier, Old Speckled Hen, Fuller's London Pride, Smithwick's Irish Ale*

   Bitters are the classic English pub drink. Low in alcohol (3–5% ABV), they are the traditional workingman's choice with a hearty pub lunch. Their hop taste is distinctively "earthy," but the hop bitterness is low, resulting in a clear and fresh-tasting beer. Bitters go well with any food, especially at lunch. They're perfect with fish and chips and great with long, intellectual conversations into the wee hours.

5. **Porters and stouts:** *Guinness,* Fuller's *London Porter,* Samuel Smith's *Taddy Porter*

   A porter is an English bitter, darker in color and stronger in alcohol, while a stout or cream porter is usually sweeter. An imperial porter has more malt and therefore a higher ABV. Porters go well with beef, while stouts and cream porters also go down well with dessert, especially chocolate cake or cheesecake.

TO YOUR HEALTH!

6. **American pale ale:** *Sierra Nevada, Three Floyds Pride & Joy,* Bell's *Pale Ale*

   Discussed in the previous lesson (Beer 101), this is a traditional American beer. A direct descendant of the English bitter, it is more highly hopped. Pale ales pair well with chicken, pork, pizza, burgers, or any American food.

7. **Brown ales:** *Newcastle Brown Ale, Goose Island Nut Brown Ale,* Dogfish Head's *Indian Brown Ale, Brooklyn Brown Ale*

   This is a diverse style, derived from the English brown ale, which itself is a derivative of the English bitter. Unlike IPAs, these beers accentuate the malt rather than the hop. Colors range from red to brown, and the flavor palate may include chocolate and caramel. Drink with any American food, including red meat, burgers, barbecue, and Cajun flavors. It works surprisingly well with Italian food.

8. **American IPA:** Dogfish Head's *60-Minute IPA* and *90-Minute IPA,* Bell's *Two Hearted Ale,* Harpoon's *Harpoon IPA,* Stone's *Stone IPA,* Three Floyds' *Alpha King,* Victory's *HopDevil*

   The IPA is the epitome of the American brewing style. Usually 6.5–7.5% ABV, IPAs have a strong hop flavor. In fact, this beer is all about the hops—the malt takes second place. Each IPA is different, ranging from high to low hoppiness; you will have to taste many of them to find the one that is best for you. A good dinner beer, IPAs pair well with meat and potatoes, shellfish, and Chinese food.

9. **Belgian ales:** *Chimay Grande Réserve, St. Bernardus Abt 12, Duvel, Orval, Trappistes Rochefort 10, Leffe Blonde Abbey Ale*

   For the sake of simplicity, we are lumping all Belgians together, but they are not all of the same style. Arising from the medieval tradition of monks brewing beer in the abbeys of Belgium, using local ingredients and wild yeast,

CHAPTER 2: THE BASICS

this class of beer has evolved into a variety of styles. The ales range from the relatively low-alcohol *Leffe Blonde Abbey Ale* (6.6% ABV) to the high-gravity *St. Bernardus Abt 12* (10% ABV). There are also fruit-flavored, sour beers (lambics), farmhouse ales, and Flemish red ales. The unifying theme is a flavor complexity due primarily to the yeast. Taste a variety of Belgian ales to appreciate the flavor, but remember to sip them from a goblet.

Belgians go well with duck, steamed mussels, cheese, charcuterie, crepes, French pastries, and appetizers. The high-alcohol variants are best enjoyed in the evening around a fireplace with someone you love.

Now that you've tasted them all, it's time to use your knowledge and go one step further, focusing your palate and developing expertise in one area. In our final lesson, we extend this approach to cover more beers and further refine your palate.

CRAFT BEER 103: HOW TO BE A BEER SNOB

3QuarksDaily.com (July 15, 2013)

The late Kingsley Amis, a noted authority on drink and a beer lover himself, acknowledged that "the best wine is much better than the best beer." However, he also pointed out that "wine is *a lot of trouble*, requiring energy and forethought." He might be pleased today to find that beer, which requires a lot less trouble, has finally come into its own.

Not long ago, beer was considered to be an uninspired, bitter-tasting beverage that was drunk in large amounts by fraternity boys and construction workers. Wine was preferred among intellectuals, the educated, and true gourmets. We struggled to learn enough about wine so as not to embarrass ourselves when presented with a wine list, and any self-made wine expert—a wine snob—was held in high regard.

But the increasing popularity of craft beer means it is now appearing on the menus of even the most discerning restaurants because it is a delightfully tasty, complex beverage that pairs well with food. So now, in addition to being able to navigate a wine list, we must learn to read a beer list.

Fortunately, it's easy to master craft beer, in part because there is a limited number of beer styles and breweries for you to re-member. Furthermore, even the most posh menu will feature only a short selection of beers, and most beers are inexpensive, in contrast to dozens of expensive wines. If you follow a few simple rules, you can quickly reach a point where you can hold your own with a beer list—or at least bluff your way through it. With a little effort, you can become recognized by your friends as one who knows craft beer, can select the best brands, and can wax eloquent about breweries and beer trivia. Yes—you, too, can become a beer snob!

First, let's define craft beer. According to the Brewer's Association, the definition of an American craft brewery is one that is "small, independent, and traditional." "Small" means an annual production of 6 million barrels of beer or less (compared to Anheuser-Busch, which sells well over 150 million barrels per year). "Independent" means that the brewery is at least 75 percent owned or controlled by a brewer, and "traditional" means that at least 50 percent of the beer it makes is all-malt beer. (Note that many mass-market beers use up to one-third rice or corn in place of the more expensive barley malt ingredients.) With a craft beer, you can be assured of quality ingredients mixed by a knowledgeable brewmaster who is motivated by taste, not just by profit.

Brewery size is important. Small breweries don't have the production capacity to have their beer distributed nationally. This is why many of them are regional—the craft beer available to me in Northeastern Pennsylvania is different from that in Chicago, for example. A microbrewery—one that produces no more than

CHAPTER 2: THE BASICS

15,000 barrels per year—is operated on an even smaller scale, often by a couple of guys working out of their garage!

Micros usually don't bottle, but they distribute their beer in kegs or serve it at their own brewpub. With limited resources for marketing and distribution, they rely heavily on word of mouth, customer loyalty, and reputation. You may have to seek out these beers, and that's where the beer snob comes in. A beer expert knows what to drink, where it came from, and how good it tastes.

Here are 10 rules for the beer snob:

1. **Drink only craft beer.**

    By avoiding mass-produced, big-label beer, you will be drinking the best-tasting beer and also supporting your regional small breweries. Be wary of "phony" craft beers, made by the large brewers to look and taste like craft beers. Some of these noncraft beers include: *Blue Moon* (MillerCoors), *Shock Top* (Anheuser-Busch), *Leinenkugel's* (SABMiller), and *Goose Island* (Anheuser-Busch). If the beer list at your restaurant or pub does not include craft beer, don't be afraid to look down your nose and tell the waiter and say, "Forget it, I'll just have water."

2. **Learn the basic beer styles.**

    To understand a beer list, you must learn to differentiate among beer styles. Here are the eight styles you should know: 1) lager (includes pilsner), 2) pale ale (American and English), 3) amber (or red or brown) ale, 4) IPA (India pale ale), 5) porter or stout, 6) Belgian ale, 7) wheat beer, and 8) saison. The easiest way to learn them is to try them. Take a trip to a bottle store and buy a representative sample of each, spend 15 minutes looking up each of them on Wikipedia, then taste and compare. Voilà! Instant expert!

3. **Know the main beer ingredients.**

    There are only three: malted barley, hops, and yeast. Malted (sprouted) barley is sweet and full of fermentable sugar. The yeast converts this sugar into alcohol and carbonation. The residual malt flavor in beer is distinctively mild and bread-like.

Hops are bitter, pungent herbs added for flavoring and used with a heavy hand in ales, especially IPAs. Hops are an acquired taste, which you really *must* acquire if you want to be a beer snob. There are many varieties of hops, but don't expect to be able to taste the differences as a novice. You can bluff your way through this by looking up the beer's website, where you may find the IBU level (International Bittering Unit, a measure of the degree of hoppiness) and the hop variety, so you can at least say something knowledgeable about the taste.

4. **Always choose draft over bottled beer.**

    Draft beer is fresh from the brewery and at the peak of flavor, whereas canned and bottled beers may deteriorate with time (remember to check the date stamp). And there is a good chance the draft list will contain a selection or two from your local microbrewery, giving you the opportunity to show off your beer expertise (see rule 6, below).

5. **Drink beer only from a glass.**

    If your beer selection is in a bottle, then insist on a glass. You would never drink wine from the bottle, so why beer? You probably won't be so fortunate as to have your beer served to you in a Spiegelau Beer Classic, a glass specifically designed to showcase hoppy American IPAs. (It's also the latest fad among beer snobs.) But at the very least, expect a standard pint glass for all beers, except for Belgian ales and high-alcohol beers, which should be served in a tulip-shaped glass.

    Drinking beer from a glass allows you to enjoy the color and clarity, to observe and then taste the frothy head, and, finally, to savor the aroma before taking a sip—while pointing out these attributes to your admiring friends.

CHAPTER 2: THE BASICS

The correct beer glass for each beer style. From left to right:
Beer mug *for American, English, and German lagers,*
Imperial pint *for English ales and stouts,*
Pilsner glass *for pilsners, light lagers, and wheat beers.*

From left to right: ***Spielgau Beer Classic*** *for American IPAs,*
Tulip glass *for barley wines, Belgian beers, and other aromatic beers,*
American pint glass *for American and English ales and lagers.*

TO YOUR HEALTH!

6. **Get to know your local craft breweries.**

    There are probably only a handful of micros and a dozen or so larger craft breweries in your area—so few that you can get to know them all! Visit a few tasting rooms and try the latest offerings. There's a good chance you'll meet an owner/brewmaster, learn his philosophy, and find out what's brewing. The true beer snob is always welcomed at his local brewery.

7. **Taste as many beers as you can, and remember the ones you like.**

    The only way to know beer is to drink it. Ask the bartender for a few tastes, purchase a sampler, or go to the local brewery tasting room. You can take notes, but it's easy to remember beer names, which are much more distinctive than wine names. For example, taste Flying Dog's *UnderDog Atlantic Lager,* Victory's *Hop-Devil IPA,* and North Coast's *Brother Thelonious.* But be careful to *taste* and not *drink* as many beers as you can. Because of their high malt content, many craft beers are high in alcohol. For example, two 7% ABV beers in standard 16-ounce draft mugs are equivalent to four 12-ounce bottles of Budweiser (4.5% ABV). Ouch!

8. **Do your homework.**

    An investment of 10 minutes online before you go out will make it easy to keep one step ahead of your friends—and even your bartender. Check what's on draft at your local beer bar and read the descriptions (Style? Hops? Aroma? Finish?). Besides the brewery websites, various Internet resources provide descriptions and objective reviews; BeerAdvocate.com is one of the oldest and most comprehensive.

    You can get a beer app for your smartphone so you'll never be caught unawares. I'm currently using Beer Citizen. Read the reviews so you can compare them to your own notes and avoid the real stinkers. Although

CHAPTER 2: THE BASICS

carefully crafted with quality ingredients, not every craft beer is delicious.

9. **Pick out a few go-to beers.**

    When you are confronted with a taproom full of unfamiliar beers, when you are facing a draft list full of mass-market lagers, or when it's pumpkin ale season (not to my taste), then stick to the old standards in bottles. Regional breweries have flagship beers that are consistently produced and readily available, so find a few that you like. My go-to beers are IPAs: Dogfish Head's *60 Minute IPA*, *Harpoon IPA*, and *Bell's Two Hearted Ale*.

10. **For extra credit, become a home brewer.**

    The best way to gain other people's respect for your beer skills is to mention that you are a home brewer. If you brew, you'll have the chance to taste and appreciate the different malts, you'll learn to tell the different hop varieties apart, and you'll be able to speak knowledgeably to a brewmaster. Alternatively, find a friend who home brews and is willing to walk you through the process, letting you try the ingredients and the final product. If all else fails and you are still motivated to taste the ingredients, you can order small amounts of hops and malted barley for just a few dollars from an online home-brewer supply store.

If you follow these easy rules, you will soon become an expert on craft beer. You may also find that you have become a true beer aficionado—seeking out unique beers, brewing your own, or even writing for a beer blog, as I do. Remember that the purpose of becoming a beer snob is to help you find and enjoy good beer. As Hunter S. Thompson wrote, "Good people drink good beer."

CHAPTER 3

BEER AND YOUR HEALTH

In this chapter, I tackle some of the health issues related to alcohol consumption, exploring whether drinking beer is good (or bad) for you. I have always been surprised by a general attitude in this country that alcohol is bad for you. I certainly did not have this perception when I lived in Europe, where a glass of beer or wine is considered a natural, healthy part of the daily diet. Perhaps it stems from our Puritan and prohibitionist roots.

I often find myself defending beer drinking against a self-righteous minority that frowns upon any alcohol consumption at all and welcomes "scientific" data that might indicate it is harmful. In reality, there is little evidence that moderate consumption of alcohol has any ill effects for the average, healthy adult. The effects of excessive alcohol consumption, on the other hand, are well-known to those of us in the health professions—and to some of our readers.

In this chapter, we'll review some of the dangers of excessive drinking and how to avoid them, with a reminder to enjoy your beer—in moderation.

IS BEER GOOD FOR YOU?

YourBeerNetwork.com (January 19, 2011)

Of course beer is healthy! When consumed in small amounts, beer adds yeast-based nutrients that our body cannot make by itself and that promote our health. This, by the way, is also true

CHAPTER 3: BEER AND YOUR HEALTH

for other yeast-based products, including wine and aged cheese. Malted barley contains a fair amount of the B vitamins—niacin, riboflavin, biotin, and folate. (You will, of course, have an adequate supply of these vitamins if you eat a balanced diet, so you don't need to get them from beer.)

Beer also contains antioxidant compounds, which help prevent cancer. Wine does, too, but perhaps the compounds are different. There is an ongoing debate as to which is healthier, beer or wine, and I won't step into that debate. But I will note that the distillation process separates alcohol from its initial fermentation mixture, so distilled spirits (whisky, vodka, etc.) do not contain the bulk of the antioxidants, vitamins, and phenolic compounds that result from malting and fermenting.

Beer is a soporific (sleeping tonic). Although alcohol itself is a mild sedative, beer seems to be stronger in this regard, and this is attributed to the hops. As an herbal supplement, hops are considered a natural sleep aid, and they're used for the treatment of insomnia. Beer also seems to be an appetite stimulant, over and above the effect of alcohol.

Overall, the major health benefit to beer drinking is in the alcohol content. There are numerous studies that show that small amounts of alcohol (1 to 3 glasses per day for men, 1 for women) reduce the risk of heart attacks, help lower cholesterol, and may help delay the age at which dementia begins. All of these studies are *epidemiological*. In other words, the studies looked at the drinking habits of large numbers of people and at average health effects relative to alcohol. They don't say much about why and how, or about the effects on individual people. Furthermore, the benefits seemed to derive from all types of alcohol; the conclusions were based on what the individual researcher wanted to study—beer or wine.

But every gift from the gods has its downside. Every adult who consumes alcoholic beverages understands that there are limits to what he or she can tolerate, and everyone knows that habitual drinking can lead to serious problems with alcoholism. A word of caution about beer drinking: as you become more sophisticated in your tastes for beer, you will probably start to drink wonderfully delightful draft beers. If so, you may find you are consuming more alcohol. For example, a pint draft (16 ounces) of *Arrogant Bastard Ale* (7.2% ABV) contains almost twice the alcohol of a 12-ounce can of *Budweiser* (5% ABV)! So if you're used to quaffing down a six-pack of *Bud*, you will end up seriously impaired if you do the same with higher-alcohol beers.

Of course beer is healthy! But it's not enough to justify heavy beer consumption or to promote beer over, say, wine. If you're looking to do either one of those, then I'm sorry, I can't help you. Instead, here's a healthy attitude: you drink beer because you like the taste, because you find it fascinating, and because it's OK to drink beer in moderate amounts.

DOES BEER MAKE YOU FAT?

YourBeerNetwork.com (June 6 and June 21, 2011)

I've heard it time and time again: beer makes you fat, and it gives you a beer belly—so don't drink it. We've already established that beer is good for you (see previous section), but does it really make you fat?

I decided to put my biochemistry background to work and get the real answer. The most logical place to start was simple dietary information on a typical beer. Just read the label, right? Wrong!

Do you ever wonder why there is no nutritional information on a beer label? Every other food and beverage you consume contains a label that tells you the exact amount of carbohydrates, protein, fat, sodium, vitamins, additives, and allergens. Even water bottles are labeled with the calorie, protein, fat, and carbs (usually 0)! Every beverage has a label—that is, except beer and wine. Why? Because beer is not a food regulated by the Food and Drug Administration (FDA), which requires nutritional labeling. Beer is regulated by the Department of Alcohol,

CHAPTER 3: BEER AND YOUR HEALTH

Tobacco, Firearms and Explosives (ATF). In fact, even the alcohol content of a beer is not on the label unless it is an import (so far as I can tell, anyway).

How frustrating to try to figure out whether or not your diet allows you to have that second pint of beer! You can get information on the calorie count of your beer, but you will have to go online to the brewery's website or check an online source for dieting and see if your beer is listed—my favorite is CalorieKing.com.

But wait—that's not the end of the story. The posted calories on those sites are not accurate, because they include calories from alcohol—and alcohol calories don't count the same way as food calories do. Not all calories are created equal!

When you consume fat, sugar, carbohydrates, or protein, the food is metabolized to completion (CO_2 and H_2O), or else it is stored as fat to be metabolized later. The calorie content of a food can be measured pretty accurately by burning it to completion in a small chamber and measuring the heat released.

But the calories measured for alcohol do not reflect how it is metabolized. That's because the alcohol you consume is not burned to completion; it is only partially metabolized. These incomplete metabolic products are not stored as fat but are lost in the urine and exhaled in your breath as acetaldehyde or acetic acid. It has been estimated that only about 16–20% of the caloric potential in alcohol is actually available to the body.

One ounce of pure alcohol has a theoretical content of 198 calories, but the body only sees about 31 of those calories. So if you want to know how many "true" calories are in your beer, you will need to look up the posted calorie content and the percentage of alcohol, calculate how much alcohol is in the volume of beer you're drinking, and then apply a correction factor.

This is my equation, using a very conservative 20% metabolism rate for beer:

True calories = (published calorie content) – (# ounces of alcohol x 160) = calories in your beer.

Let's look at two examples, using published calories from CalorieKing.com:

1. 12 ounces of *Guinness*, listed at 126 calories.

   At 4% ABV, the glass holds 0.48 ounces of alcohol. Corrected calories: 126 − (0.48 x 160) = 126 − 76.8 = 50 calories.

2. 12 ounces of *Samuel Adams Boston Lager*, listed at 180 calories.

   At 5% ABV, the glass contains 0.6 ounces of alcohol. Corrected calories: 180 − (0.6 x 160) = 180 − 96 = 94 calories.

That's not too bad, is it? Much better than a sweetened martini, a piña colada, or even a Coke.

Good luck trying to solve the equation after a couple of pints. Forget it. Just go ahead and have the next one.

So why does beer make me fat if the calories are so low?

In the previous subsection, we discussed how beer has a lot fewer calories than you think. So why do so many people get fat drinking beer? Let's take a closer look at beer as a food.

The nutritional components of beer come from malt. Malt contains starches, sugars, protein, B vitamins, sodium, and potassium. After fermentation, all the sugars are converted by the yeast into alcohol, leaving behind starch, protein, B vitamins, and salts. What's left is the equivalent of white bread. An average 12-ounce beer has about the same nutritional value as a slice of white bread.

Even better than white bread, beer contains no fat, no cholesterol, and no sugar. The major source of calories in beer is the carbohydrates, specifically starches. A 12-ounce average beer contains about 10–15 grams (g) of carbohydrates, depending on how much malted barley or other grain was used to produce it. Maltier beers, such as lagers, have more carbs. High-alcohol beers and barley wines also start with more malt, but very high-alcohol beers have added sugar, which is used up by fermenta-

CHAPTER 3: BEER AND YOUR HEALTH

tion with proportionally less carb content, especially if served in a small glass.

What does this mean to your diet?

1. Beer is fat-free.
2. Beer is sugar-free. The only exceptions are milk stouts, some of which contain lactose, which is added for sweetening and which yeast can't digest (and which many humans can't digest, either).
3. Drinking one average beer is equivalent to drinking a jigger of bourbon (40% ABV) and having a slice of white bread, with no butter.
4. *But*, beer is high in carbs. A single 12-ounce pour of *Samuel Adams Boston Lager* has 18 g of carbs, and one 12-ounce pour of *Guinness* has 10 g. If you are sensitive to carbs, or if you're following a low-carb diet (e.g., the South Beach Diet, the Atkins Diet), you will probably gain weight drinking beer, just the same as you would eating bread. So skip the bread, skip the beer, and drink a bourbon instead.

It's really hard to integrate beer into a low-carb diet. One option is to drink a low-carb beer. For example, a 12-ounce bottle of *Michelob ULTRA* has 95 calories, has 2.6 g of carbs, and is 4.2% ABV. Compare it to a 12-ounce pour of *Samuel Adams* (18 g carb) or *Guinness* (10 g carb). You will note this beer is very low on hops and has almost no malt flavor, but at least you can drink it on a low-carb diet. You may end up drinking three or four to feel as if you really had a beer, and then you're really not ahead of the game.

Another alternative is to drink a barley wine; that is, a very strong beer with a high alcohol content. Most bartenders will give you a small pour rather than a pint. For example, a 6-ounce pour of Bell's *Hopslam Ale*, 10% ABV, has 44 "true calories" and 6 g of carbs. It's very satisfying if you sip it slowly.

Why, then, does beer make you fat? It's not the beer—it's everything else you eat when drinking beer. Hops act as an appetite stimulant, as does alcohol. After a couple of beers, I find it hard to resist the salty popcorn that every bar seems to provide gratis. That's 200 calories for a small basket of popcorn, 300 calories for a slice of pepperoni pizza, and over 1,000 calories for an 8-ounce bag of potato chips. And if you are pairing beer with bacon and charcuterie, all bets are off. It takes moderation and willpower.

Yes, it is possible. I drink beer and I'm not fat.

ALCOHOL, PART 1: YOUR BRAIN ON BEER

YourBeerNetwork.com (October 18, 2011)

Why is it that some people can drink pint after pint of beer without getting wasted while someone else will fall over after one drink? Today, we're going to answer this question. We'll discuss alcohol intoxication and give you a few tips on how to handle more beer with less drunkenness.

First, let's dispel a misconception. It's *not true* that some people tolerate a higher blood alcohol level than others. With few exceptions, everyone reaches the same level of intoxication at the same blood alcohol concentration (BAC). Table 2 gives the level of intoxication at each of several BACs. You can see that most casual drinkers stay within the 0.01–0.10% range, while the first-time drinker or serious binger might be well over 0.2% for a time. You'll rarely see anyone over 0.3%, though a chronic alcoholic may still be conscious with a BAC over 0.4%! The legal limit in most states is 0.08%, but you'll want to keep yours well below that for safety and optimal enjoyment.

Here's what you need to know. The highest BAC you can reach with a single drink is related only to your weight. If you were to give all the alcohol in a pint of 5% ABV beer (0.8 ounces of alcohol) rapidly by IV to an average 180-pound man, he would reach a BAC of about 0.05%. On the other hand, if you were to do the same to a 90-pound woman, she would reach twice that

CHAPTER 3: BEER AND YOUR HEALTH

BAC, or 0.1%. But have them each *drink* the two beers instead and the BAC will be lower for both. How much lower is almost impossible to predict since there is tremendous variability from person to person.

Since everyone has the same level of intoxication at a given BAC, the difference in alcohol tolerance is not due only to *how much* you consume but also to how your body handles the alcohol. The latter is determined only by two things: (1) how quickly the alcohol goes in and (2) how rapidly it goes out. Once you understand those factors, you can use them to your advantage and improve your alcohol tolerance.

1. **How Quickly Alcohol Goes In.** About 70 percent of the alcohol you drink is absorbed directly by the stomach, and the rest is absorbed by the intestine. Pure alcohol is absorbed rapidly on an empty stomach, reaching its peak blood level in a half hour. If alcohol absorption goes on over a longer period of time, the body will have time to remove alcohol before it reaches its peak level. Alcohol absorption is slowed down by food in the stomach, including beer itself. Eating a meal while drinking is the best way to slow absorption of alcohol, and those pretzels, popcorn, and chips help a little if you fill up *before* you drink, not after. Worth remembering.

2. **How Quickly Alcohol is Removed.** There is tremendous variation from one person to another in alcohol metabolism, and this accounts for the major difference in alcohol tolerance. Alcohol is metabolized through its conversion to acetaldehyde in the liver by an enzyme called ADH (alcohol dehydrogenase). Acetaldehyde might make your breath smell like a drunk's or give you a headache, nausea, or a hangover—but it is not intoxicating. The more rapid your metabolism, the lower BAC you achieve with a drink.

Alcohol is metabolized at a constant rate, regardless of your BAC or how much you consume. This rate is determined only by the amount of ADH in your liver. The ADH level varies tremendously from person to person, and it is the primary determinant of who can hold their liquor and who can't. A person with an average metabolism can clear 0.015–0.02% of blood alcohol per hour—that's about one-third to one-half of a beer per hour.

Seasoned drinkers can do better, and chronic alcoholics can double or triple that rate—unless they have damaged their livers to the point of cirrhosis, when ADH drops to a very low level. An experienced drinker will develop a feel for his or her alcohol metabolic rate and can achieve a *steady state*, wherein the amount consumed is equal to the amount removed by the body. The key, then, is to increase your alcohol metabolism so your steady-state rate increases.

The good news is that you can gradually raise the level of ADH in your liver; the bad news is that it takes days or weeks to increase. Regular consumption of alcohol is the best way to increase your liver enzymes—for this purpose, daily consumption is better than binge drinking. Some medications will increase your ADH, as will some medical conditions. Estrogens and androgens increase your ADH, so levels drop as we age and hormones decline.

This decline in ADH levels lowers our tolerance for alcohol. Menopause and "man-o-pause" are curses to the beer drinker. Ironically, pregnant women have very high levels of ADH and, in theory, can metabolize alcohol faster than they could before they were pregnant—even though they don't drink at all.

Putting it all together, here is the Beer Doctor's advice on how to hold your beer:

1. Don't drink on an empty stomach. Eat first and keep food in your stomach if you're planning to drink a lot.

2. Don't chug your beer, especially if you're not eating. If you're thirsty, fill up on water or soft drinks first or start with a light beer.

CHAPTER 3: BEER AND YOUR HEALTH

3. Pace yourself, keeping an eye on the beer's alcohol content, and try not to exceed your body's metabolic rate.

4. Remember that your alcohol level will continue to go up if you're drinking with food in your stomach, so keep count and slow down if necessary.

5. Increase your tolerance by gradually increasing your alcohol consumption over a few days to weeks. This will raise your ADH.

But—what if you miscalculate? Suppose you find you've had too much to drink and want to sober up. Sadly, there is no way to get alcohol out of your system once it is in your blood—short of kidney dialysis. If there is still alcohol in your stomach, vomiting will get rid of it and keep your alcohol level from going higher. Black coffee, aspirin, water, salty food—you name it—nothing lowers your BAC except your own liver, which goes at its own pace. All you can do is wait or sleep it off until your blood level drops at a rate of about one-half beer per hour. Keep up with fluids since alcohol makes you pretty dehydrated, which will worsen your inevitable hangover.

Table 2: Level of Intoxication by Blood Alcohol Concentration (BAC)

BAC	Intoxication Level
0.01–0.10%	Euphoria (happiness, a "high"), slight loss of coordination and attention span
0.11–0.2%	Some loss of coordination and balance, poor attention, impaired judgment, slurred speech, mood swings
0.21–0.3%	Severe loss of coordination, incoherent thoughts, confusion, nausea, and vomiting
0.31–0.4%	Drowsiness, memory lapse, loss of consciousness; similar to surgical anesthesia
over 0.4%	Severe alcohol poisoning, slowed or stopped breathing, coma, and death

What about your drinking companions? If you notice that someone is excessively intoxicated, you will, of course, make sure he doesn't drive, and you should also keep him from drinking any more alcohol. Get him to a safe place to sleep it off, and make sure he is well-hydrated. Be concerned if you see signs of alcohol poisoning. If he passes out and you can't wake him up, then you may need to take him to a hospital for medical treatment. Hopefully, neither you nor your drinking companions will ever reach that condition.

ALCOHOL, PART 2: SOME SOBERING THOUGHTS

YourBeerNetwork.com (November 11, 2011)

Up till now, we've been singing the praises of beer. But as you know, drinking has its dark side.

Picture the lovable old drunk. He's sitting at the bar, sipping his beer, telling funny stories that he seems to be making up as he goes along. His speech is a bit slurred, his eyes are shaky, and he's a bit unsteady on his feet. Maybe he's just had a bit too much tonight, but he's a great guy—everybody's friend—and he doesn't seem to be having any problems at all.

Right? Wrong! This man has a lot of problems! He is showing the classic signs of Korsakoff's syndrome, an incurable brain disease caused by a lack of vitamin B6 (thiamine). It's hard to imagine anyone with a vitamin deficiency nowadays, but chronic alcoholics are especially susceptible to B6 deficiency because they may go for days "drinking their dinner," without eating any fresh produce. Also, alcohol interferes with absorption of B6. Thiamine is necessary for brain metabolism, and the parts of the brain necessary for coordination of speech, vision, balance, and memory are affected the most.

CHAPTER 3: BEER AND YOUR HEALTH

The classic Korsakoff person shuffles with legs spread wide, falls frequently, slurs his speech, and may have very shaky, wandering eyes. And, of course, he has memory problems.

One of the most fascinating (and endearing) symptoms of Korsakoff's syndrome is called "confabulation," or falsification of memories, in which a person makes up stories about his past, which he can't remember. Combine this with slurred speech and an outgoing personality and you get the lovable old drunk from TV and the movies.

During my hospital residency, every suspected alcoholic had a yellow intravenous bag drip—the color was due to thiamine, added to help prevent Korsakoff's syndrome. When you saw a patient with a yellow IV, you knew he was an alcoholic. It was also a tip-off to watch out for the DTs.

We've all heard the term "the DTs" and know it stands for *delirium tremens,* but you probably don't know what it means—other than the fact that it's the name of a delightful, high-alcohol Belgian beer with a pink elephant on the label. The DTs are the symptoms of alcohol withdrawal.

In a chronic alcoholic who stops drinking, the DTs usually start about two days after the last drink. "Delirium" refers to mental confusion, and "tremens" refers to shaking or convulsions—both of which are exactly what happens. The delirium almost always includes disorientation, confusion, and hallucinations, while the tremors go along with restlessness, fever, and sweating. Eventually, full convulsions may occur. It's not pretty.

The DTs are serious business. They are treated in a hospital intensive care unit, using sedatives and antiseizure medications, and they take about a week to resolve. Most alcoholics know that you can prevent the shakes if you have another drink, but this only delays the inevitable. If you come across someone who you think has the DTs, *do not give him a drink!* Get him to a hospital, because the DTs can be fatal!

So what about those pink elephants, anyway? Jack London was the first one to use the term in his 1913 autobiographical novel *John Barleycorn.* He described Barleycorn as "the man whom we all know, stupid, unimaginative, whose brain is bitten numbly by numb maggots ... who sees, in the extremity of his ecstasy, blue mice and pink elephants. He is the type that gives rise to the jokes in the funny papers."

Hallucinations are common with many recreational drugs during the high, but with alcohol, hallucinations occur *after* the high is over, along with withdrawal. Hallucinations during the DTs are visual but also tactile; they give you the feeling that something is crawling on your skin. Ugh.

More common than the DTs, and much less-often fatal, is *alcoholic hallucinosis*, which starts 12 to 24 hours after drinking stops. Unlike a drunk who has the DTs, the hallucinating drunk is conversant, conscious, and oriented, and he fully believes his hallucinations are real. The apparitions are usually visual and auditory, most commonly taking the form of accusing or threatening voices. They may be accompanied by a Disneyesque soundtrack as the pink elephants float by. Fortunately, this condition is self-limited, and unlike the DTs, it won't kill you.

But there are other fatal complications of excessive drinking, such as liver damage. The liver filters out all the alcohol you drink, and it can get hit pretty hard by a big drinking binge. The result may be a few days of *alcoholic hepatitis*, with belly pain, nausea, and jaundice (yellow skin and eyes). Alcoholic hepatitis is not fatal and will resolve in a few days, but chronic drinking can also lead to permanent liver damage in the form of cirrhosis of the liver—and advanced cirrhosis can be fatal.

In *alcoholic cirrhosis*, the liver does not function properly. It can't process your food, leading to jaundice and weight loss. It stops making blood-clotting factors, and you become a bleeder. It can't drain the abdomen, and fluid builds up. Ever see a guy with a big, swollen belly, skinny arms, and yellow skin? That's the classic picture of cirrhosis—though, in all fairness, there are other causes of cirrhosis besides drinking. Cirrhosis doesn't go away, and it can kill you. If you develop it, you might be waiting a long time for a liver transplant.

Unfortunately, you don't have to be a frank alcoholic or even a drunk to develop cirrhosis. You just need to drink. A lot. Daily. This is probably why the French have a much higher rate

CHAPTER 3: BEER AND YOUR HEALTH

of cirrhosis than Americans do—as a nation, they drink a lot of wine with almost every meal. However, they're rarely intoxicated. Estimates are that having three to four or more drinks per day increases the chance of cirrhosis, if it's kept up over a decade or more.

Where does that leave us? Are we ready to take The Pledge and give up alcohol completely? I hope not. The purpose of this section is not to dissuade you from drinking but to give you enough knowledge to understand what it means to drink responsibly—and to help your friends do the same.

DOES BEER CAUSE CANCER?

3QuarksDaily.com (February 24, 2014)

I have been taken to task by several of my readers for promoting beer drinking. I've been asked, "How can you, a cancer doctor, advocate drinking beer, when it is KNOWN to cause cancer?" So it's time to set the facts straight. Is moderate beer drinking good for your health, as I have always maintained, or does it cause cancer?

Recently, there has been some discussion in the popular press about studies showing a possible link between alcohol and cancer. As a matter of fact, reports linking foods to cancer causation (or prevention) are relatively common. I generally ignore these press releases because they generate a lot of hype but are usually based on single studies that, on follow-up, turn out to have flaws or cannot be confirmed. However, the negative follow-up study rarely receives any publicity. Moreover, there are often other studies published at other times showing completely contradictory results. For example, studies have shown that red wine both prevents and causes cancer.

Furthermore, there is a great deal of self-righteousness about certain foods, and this attitude can cloud objectivity and lead to bias in interpreting the results. Often, these feelings have strong political implications as well. Some politically charged dietary issues include vegetarianism, the growing of genetically modified crops, the use of artificial sweeteners, and the consumption of sugared soft drinks.

Alcohol fits right into this category—remember, we are the country that adopted Prohibition for 13 years. There is no doubt the United States has significant public health issues related to alcohol use—including alcohol-related auto accidents, underage drinking, and alcoholism—and the consequent problems of unemployment, cirrhosis of the liver, brain and neurological problems, and fetal alcohol syndrome. Wouldn't it be great if the government could mandate a label on every beer can stating, "Consumption of alcohol can cause cancer and should be avoided"? Wouldn't that be a wonderful "I told you so!" for the alcohol-causes-cancer naysayers!

Before going further, I will acknowledge that there *are* alcohol-related cancers. As a specialist, I am well aware that cancers of the head and neck area, the larynx (voice box), and the esophagus are frequently seen in heavy drinkers, almost always in association with cigarette smoking. Liver cancer is seen primarily in people with cirrhosis—also a result of heavy drinking.

In both cases, the more alcohol that is consumed, the greater the risk of developing one of these cancers—and I have rarely seen these cancers in nonsmokers or nondrinkers. But assuming that my readers are not alcoholics, the question that they are really asking is whether or not *they* are going to get cancer from low to moderate beer drinking.

So what, then, are the facts? Does beer cause cancer? This is a much more difficult question to answer than most people realize, and it can easily be the subject of years of study for a PhD dissertation (and probably has been). Researchers will be quick to admit how difficult it is to do scientifically rigorous studies on the health effects of individual dietary components. You can't just take a group of 30-year-olds, split them into two groups, give beer to one group and make the other abstain, watch them for 20 years, and see who gets more cancer.

CHAPTER 3: BEER AND YOUR HEALTH

So we have to rely on population studies—estimating alcohol consumption based on purchasing statistics, self-reporting of drinking (which is often unreliable), surveys, and death certificates for cancer. Incidentally, beer is not considered separately from other alcoholic beverages in any of these studies.

For example, an interesting study by Holahan and colleagues, published in 2010 in the journal *Alcoholism: Clinical and Experimental Research*, followed 1,824 middle-aged men and women (ages 55–65) over 20 years and found that moderate drinkers lived longer than did both heavy drinkers and teetotalers. In particular, their data suggested that nondrinkers had a 50% higher death rate than did moderate drinkers (meaning people who have 1–2 drinks per day).

Others have criticized this conclusion because the no-alcohol group included people who didn't drink because they were already at a higher risk of death for other reasons (such as serious medical conditions or previous cancers) and because it also included former alcoholics who were on the wagon. The authors claimed that they controlled for these variables, but that is almost impossible to do, which is one of the reasons why it is so difficult to get accurate data from this kind of study. So while it may be hard to conclude from this study that moderate drinking increases your life span, it is fair to conclude that moderate drinking doesn't shorten it.[1]

What about cancer? The publication that started the most recent hype about cancer and alcohol appeared in the April 2013 issue of *The American Journal of Public Health* and was written by David Nelson MD, MPH, and his colleagues. They combined information from others' publications with epidemiological surveys to determine the number of cancer deaths attributable to alcohol, as well as the types of cancer that were associated.

They found that about 3 percent of all cancer deaths in the U.S. were related to alcohol consumption, with most of it seen in the head and neck, larynx, and esophagus. There was a slightly increased risk observed at low alcohol use (greater than no drinks but less than one-and-a-half drinks per day), which led them to conclude that "regular alcohol use at low consumption levels is also associated with increased cancer risk." I looked at their study and couldn't argue with their conclusion, but I don't think the risk is significant enough to recommend becoming a teetotaler.[2]

Neither does the National Cancer Institute (NCI, at http://www.cancer.gov/). Heavy drinking aside, the NCI does not recommend that people discontinue low or moderate drinking, since it would have only a minimal impact on their chance of developing cancer. Some caution is indicated for specific cancers: there is a 50 percent increased risk of breast cancer in women who drink more than 3 drinks per day compared to nondrinkers; similarly, the risk of colon cancer is increased by 50 percent in people who drink more than 3.5 drinks per day.

Incidentally, 3.5 drinks per day is still well above the level that is considered low to moderate drinking, which is usually defined as no more than 1 drink per day for a woman or 2 per day for a man. That being said, lowering your alcohol consumption deserves some consideration if you are anxious to change your odds for these two specific cancers. Nonetheless, the risks from alcohol are still low when compared to the impact of other lifestyle factors. Addressing these factors will have a much greater impact than giving up that beer or wine with your dinner. In other words, don't smoke; lose weight if you are overweight; exercise; eat a high-fiber diet; increase your vegetable and fruit consumption while limiting red meat; avoid processed food; and follow up on your doctor's cancer-screening recommendations for colonoscopy, pap smears, mammography, and prostate screening.

Do the positive effects of drinking beer outweigh the negative effects? Moderate alcohol consumption has been reported to lower the risks of heart disease, stroke, hypertension, and type 2 diabetes. For men, it may lower the risk of kidney stones and prostate cancer, it may improve bone health, and it may prevent brain-function decline. Alcohol consumption actually lowers the risk of kidney cancer and lymphoma. Overall, in most studies, the positive effect was very small, but the beneficial effects of beer are only in moderate drinking—there are none for those

CHAPTER 3: BEER AND YOUR HEALTH

who drink to excess. And of course, there are social and psychological benefits to sharing a beer with friends.

So, is beer drinking good for you? Or is it bad? Are you healthier if you drink, say, a beer or two per day, or are you worse off? My conclusion as a medical specialist is this: it depends. On average, for the general population, drinking a little alcohol is better than abstaining completely. But on an individual basis, it depends on your current health conditions and your risk factors. Are you more likely to die of heart disease or of colon cancer? And if you want to cut down your risk of either condition, you must be sure to avoid cigarettes, keep your weight down, exercise, eat a high-fiber diet low in red meat and processed foods, and increase your fruit and vegetable intake. The impact of alcohol consumption is likely to be small compared to these lifestyle changes.

What does the Beer Doctor do? As a cancer specialist, my lifestyle includes all of the above recommendations on exercise, weight, and diet. I continue to enjoy my beer, but I keep my consumption within the low-to-moderate range, that is, on average about 0.5 to 1 per day—and not every day. For me, the health benefits of drinking beer outweigh the negatives. To your health!

---

[1] Charles J. Holahan et al., "Late-Life Alcohol Consumption and 20-Year Mortality," *Alcoholism: Clinical and Experimental Research* 34, no. 11 (2010): 1961–1971.

[2] David E. Nelson et al., "Alcohol-Attributable Cancer Deaths and Years of Potential Life Lost in the United States," *American Journal of Public Health* 103, no. 4 (2013): 641–648.

Three Lithuanians sharing a beer in Wilkes-Barre, Pennsylvania's Rolling Mill Hill neighborhood, about 1903. Rick's Grandfather Gober is the man in the middle.

CHAPTER 4

OUR REGIONAL BEERS: NORTHEASTERN PENNSYLVANIA

Every community has its common culture, its regional accents, its "-isms"—and increasingly today, its regional breweries. Although I am a relative newcomer to NEPA—as we residents of Northeastern Pennsylvania refer to our area—I feel very much at home here, perhaps because it has a lot in common with the area where I grew up.

Beer is one of those common threads. In this chapter, I will share my experiences and impressions of the craft beer scene in NEPA and nearby areas. I will also introduce you to the unique dialect and quirky customs of our area, and you can judge for yourself how they complement each other.

Although you may never have an opportunity to visit NEPA and taste our beers, this chapter will give you an idea of how the local craft brew scene is developing, as well as its impact on regional America. And it may give you an incentive to come on out and visit.

TO YOUR HEALTH!

DARE BEER'S GOOD IN DEH VALLEY, HEYNIT?

(Translation: Their beer is good in the Wyoming Valley, isn't it?)

YourBeerNetwork.com (May 13, 2012)

Confused? We were speaking Heyna, the local dialect here in the anthracite coal country of NEPA. The valley we are referring to is the Wyoming Valley of the great Susquehanna River, located where it winds its way between the Poconos and the Appalachian Mountains.

The dialect is an amalgam of a second-generation European immigrant accent (where "th" is never uttered) and blue-collar slang, softened by Pennsylvania Dutch ("ain't it?" = "heyna?"), with some Pittsburgh phrases thrown in and a few unexpected surprises, such as "haitch" for *h* and "chimley" for "chimney." It's one of the few regional dialects that is still alive and thriving—and so is the regional beer scene where Heyna is spoken.

Recently, I left Goshen, Indiana, and I moved my medical practice to Wilkes-Barre, NEPA. Why and how is a story for another time. I did not move here for the beer, but I could have. This is a great place for the beer lover! In addition to great beer bars (which I will cover in a future article), there are a surprising number of good breweries in the area. It was a stroke of luck that the First Annual Electric City Craft Brew Fest was held within a month of my arrival here, giving me the opportunity to taste microbrews and meet the brewers.

As brewfests go, this one was pretty nice. There were about 40 featured breweries, mostly from Pennsylvania or nearby. It was a good-sized crowd, but the Fest was not oversold, so I was able to taste everything on my list, and (almost) nothing ran out. The pours were generous. The food vendors sold good-value, beer-friendly local food: barbecue pork sandwiches, brats, pierogies, crab cakes, french fries, and jerky. Rock music played by a DJ added to the festive atmosphere, though at times it was difficult to have a conversation.

CHAPTER 4: OUR REGIONAL BEERS: NEPA

To get the most out of this brewfest, I concentrated on regional breweries within 50 to 70 miles of home, giving me the opportunity to taste small-batch beer, which I can't buy in stores (though it may be on draft at local pubs). Some small-batch beers are not even handled by distributors, and so the breweries do their own distribution. The 50-mile limit excluded the bigger regional breweries, many of which are excellent.

My general conclusion is that the craft breweries in this area are quite good because they have a discerning and divided audience. The Valley has both lager lovers and hopheads who are adamant about their preferences, so you don't see the kind of overspecialization that you see in, for example, the Chicago lagers or the West Coast hop houses. Myself, I appreciate the hoppy ales, and I have been impressed with the well-balanced use of hops that I believe characterizes high-IBU beers in Pennsylvania. I'm not a judge of lagers, though I enjoy them.

I tasted everything on my list. When I found a beer I really liked, I made it a point to ask the brewers at the festival what hops they used, since I'm a home brewer myself and am always interested. In general, I found that, compared to Midwestern and West Coast beers, the use of strong American C hops (Cascade, Chinook, Centennial, etc.) is throttled back; I saw more European and English hops in these beers. An overly hopped IPA can be very unpleasant, and very few brewers know how to balance it with a good malt selection or other ingredients. Here in NEPA, they seem to mostly get it right.

Of the beers sampled, here are my picks:

Best of show: *Ladder Dive Rye IPA*
   3 Guys & A Beer'd Brewing Company

Second place: *Bourbon Barrel Porter*
   ShawneeCraft Brewing Company

Last place: *Hops'olutely*
   Fegley's BrewWorks

With that introduction, here's a summary of my tasting of strictly local beers at the 2012 First Annual Electric City Craft Brew Fest, almost alphabetically by brewery:

TO YOUR HEALTH!

Breaker Brewing Company, Wilkes-Barre, Pennsylvania

If you don't know what a breaker is, then you're not from around here. A breaker is a multistory building where newly mined coal is crushed and sorted by size. Though anthracite coal has not been mined in the Valley since 1959—when the Susquehanna flooded the entire system of deep mines—abandoned breakers and a few bootleg mines still dot the landscape.

And we Valley residents are proud of this heritage, as almost everyone had a grandpa, father, or uncle who worked the mines and brought his lunch pail home at the end of the day to fill it with beer at one of the many local saloons along the way. So we naturally take to a brewery at which coal mining inspires and names the beers.

I believe that's one reason Breaker Brewing is growing in popularity and distribution. The other reason is they make good beer. I spoke with Mark, one of the owners, who explained that they are making traditional beers—but each with a unique twist. I had tasted some of their beers in local taverns, and some were a bit rough, but their IPA is exceptional. *I Love PA* (I♥PA) is extremely well-hopped with American C hops, and it's now my pick at local pubs.

Barley Creek Brewing Company, Tannersville, Pennsylvania

This is a very small outfit that makes excellent beer—but sadly for me, they are a brewpub, and they only sell their beer on-site or in growlers (a container of beer). They cater to the outdoorsy trade—fishers, hunters, and skiers—and their beers are aptly named. I tasted their *Angler Black Lager*, a German-style dunkel, which was very drinkable and nicely done.

Fegley's BrewWorks, Allentown, Pennsylvania

I tried their *Hop'solutely*, a tripel IPA. This is a high-alcohol beer (11.5% ABV), bottled with a cork and cage, like a fancy Belgian. This one has a potpourri of strong, citrusy American hops: Summit, Amarillo, Chinook, and Cascade. Though you need an assertive hop blend to soften the alcohol, more is not necessarily

CHAPTER 4: OUR REGIONAL BEERS: NEPA

better. Though I am a hophead, this beer missed the mark. Can you have too many hops? Hop'solutely.

Stegmaier (Lion Brewery), Wilkes-Barre, Pennsylvania

Lion is a huge brewery, and it is at ground zero in the Valley. Although not a craft brewery (the total production is much larger than craft), *Stegmaier* is their craft line. They tend toward lagers, but they make a creditable IPA that is pretty much available anywhere in NEPA, and it goes well with food. It's my drink of choice when I'm at a restaurant where the only other options are mass-market lagers. It's solid and predictable, though technically not a craft beer.

ShawneeCraft Brewing Company, Shawnee on Delaware, Pennsylvania

This is a brewery to keep your eye on. Their beers are wonderfully unique, and they have a commitment to (mostly) organic production and low environmental impact. As a result, they will probably not grow in volume or distribution, which apparently is OK with the owner, who is brewing because he loves it. (He still has a day job.) And you can't beat the location in the Delaware Valley. But their beer is hard to find outside of Scranton.

Their *Apiarius* pale ale is brewed with honey from the brewery's own hives. They are also growing raspberries for their upcoming framboise. And the most sophisticated beer I tasted at the brewfest was their *Bourbon Barrel Porter*: It has 10.5% ABV, with a modest IBU of 33 and 95% organic content. Barrel aging is the latest fad in craft beers, but this one actually tastes great; it was hard to stop drinking it.

3 Guys & A Beer'd Brewing Company, Carbondale, Pennsylvania

This is one of the newest breweries on the scene, open only since early 2012, "up da line" in Carbondale.

I have rarely seen a rye beer, and the ones I've tasted tended to be more "interesting" than "tasty." But their *Ladder Dive Rye IPA* was outstanding. I could drink it all afternoon, and I almost did.

I was also fortunate to get a taste of their new Chocolate Porter, which was a special release for the brewfest and which is also available seasonally, November through January. It is a very dark porter that has a distinctive chocolate taste, probably from the added cocoa. I'm not usually a fan of flavored beers, but this one was quite drinkable and very reminiscent of *Guinness.*

Keep your eye on this brewery. I think their master brewer has a wonderful palate—as well as a red beard. Too bad about the name.

Yuengling, Pottsville, Pennsylvania

Yuengling claims to be the oldest continuously operating brewery in the United States; like most large breweries, their roots are in German lagers, and *Yuengling Traditional Lager* is a staple throughout the state. Strictly speaking, they are technically not a craft brewery, because their volume is too high at 2.5 million barrels and their flagship beer is not all malt. But their beer is good and always available. I tasted the *Lord Chesterfield Ale,* a good copy of an English bitter. It's available everywhere.

Just for the record, I did taste quite a few other beers beyond my imposed 50-mile limit. Some of the highlights are as follows:

Tröegs Brewing (Hershey, Pennsylvania) featured their flagship *HopBack Amber Ale,* which uses a unique hopping process. Before fermentation, the wort is passed through the hopback vessel, which recirculates through fresh hops, extracting more flavor. (Think of it as a tea bag.) The taste is sublime—highly recommended.

The Victory Brewing Company (Downingtown, Pennsylvania) *Hop Devil IPA* is always a favorite, and **Yards Brewing Company** (Philadelphia, Pennsylvania) *Philadelphia Pale Ale* is a great IPA. I consider the **Dogfish Head** (Milton, Delaware) *90 minute* and *60 minute* IPAs to be the king of East Coast hops. True to form, they presented a *Demo IPA,* a surprisingly tasty, hoppy black IPA. Keep your eyes open for this one! I hope they expand production. It's a keeper.

CHAPTER 4: OUR REGIONAL BEERS: NEPA

I left the brewfest full of pierogies, crab cakes, hops, and good cheer. The festival whetted my appetite to spend more time at the local brew houses in my new home town of Wilkes-Barre, Pennsylvania. Lotsa good beer on tap, more in bottles. Lotsa good taverns up and down da line, heynit?

BEER IN THE VALLEY

YourBeerNetwork.com (January 9, 2013)

There are no gastropubs in the Valley. *Every* pub serves good food—often homemade and usually available until late. That's just the way things are here in Luzerne County, Pennsylvania, in the Wyoming Valley of the Susquehanna River in NEPA. It's one of the many delights of living in da Valley, as I learned shortly after moving here.

Luzerne County is home to about 320,000 people living in 76 different municipalities. There are 489 churches and many more bars, brewpubs, taverns, and saloons. How many bars are there? The Commonwealth of Pennsylvania limits the number of bar licenses in any county to 1 per 3,000 of population, but it seems to me that there are more than 106 bars in the Valley. That's because there are more than 106 street corners where bars are located, and there are more bars than churches (I did a quick head count once). Both bar and restaurant liquor licenses require food service on the premises, which explains why every bar serves food.

The Valley is a well-kept secret. Less than 120 miles from two major metropolitan centers (New York and Philadelphia) and nestled among the ski resorts and casinos of the Poconos, it is a provincial place where things change slowly or not at all. It reminds me of Chicago in the 1950s, where I grew up. My Chicago was a city of small neighborhoods, centered on ethnic churches (Polish, Bohemian, Italian, Irish, Lithuanian, etc.) and the corner bar. That Chicago is gone, along with its corner bars. But it is alive and well in the Valley. I feel right at home here.

TO YOUR HEALTH!

Those ethnic Europeans drank a lot of alcohol! They were coal miners, tradesmen, and factory workers. After a long day at work, they'd stop at the corner for a drink and fill their lunch pails with beer to bring home for dinner. When the mines flooded in 1959 and coal mining ended, the miners had to leave the Valley for work elsewhere. Many former residents are now moving back and finding that the work may have changed but that the good food and the beer tradition remain.

My husband, Rick, grew up around here, and he can point out watering holes where he drank when he was in college. For instance, Senunas' (a Lithuanian name), adjacent to King's College, serves hearty, home-cooked food to hungry students during the day and hosts a boisterous college crowd at night.

The corner bars in Wilkes-Barre, Luzerne, and Kingston have changed little in 50 years. Many have changed hands, changed names, and acquired a new coat of paint, but they are all still pretty much as they were 50 to 100 years ago. What has changed, though, is the interest in craft beers. Many bars offer a selection of regional craft beers (e.g., beers from Dogfish Head, Victory, and Yuengling); a variety of American and international bottles; and beer from small, independent, local breweries.

Craft beers abound in the area. There are over 111 licensed breweries in Pennsylvania, of which 8 are located in NEPA alone. There are also the nearby East Coast breweries such as Dogfish Head. It's fun to track down new releases from these breweries; the website MyBeerBuzz.com tells you what's "on" at various drinking establishments—very convenient for the craft-draft hunter such as myself.

It can be a challenge to taste these wonderful brews since the Commonwealth of Pennsylvania is an alcoholic beverage–control state. By law, beer may be purchased from a licensed beer store in cases or kegs, usually from large breweries. If you prefer smaller amounts of craft beer, you will have to buy it at a food establishment. Bottled beer is available for carryout in many delis, pizza parlors, and bars, and good selections of craft beer are available in the larger supermarkets that maintain restaurant areas. Carryout is limited to 192 ounces per purchase;

CHAPTER 4: OUR REGIONAL BEERS: NEPA

larger amounts require multiple trips to your car, carrying two six-packs each trip.

But if you want to taste the local craft beers, visiting a drinking establishment is your best choice since the draft beer is fresh, you can drink as much as you like, and you can enjoy the camaraderie of like-minded individuals. The best beer bars have extensive collections of U.S. and imported bottles, more so than you might find in comparable establishments in other states. My current regional favorites are Breaker Brewing Company's *Phoebe Snow White IPA* and Susquehanna Brewing's *HopFive IPA*.

Bar patrons in the Valley expect quite a bit more than burgers, fries, and nachos. The gamut runs from Mom-and-Pop cafes—which serve home-cooked, fabulous dinners with daily specials—to foodie bars with gourmet chefs. Typical bar food in the Valley includes (1) seafood: lobster tails, oysters, steamed clams, fried haddock, and shrimp; (2) ethnic food: potato pancakes, pierogies, stuffed cabbage, homemade sausage, lasagna, and pasta; (3) healthy salads and vegetarian entrees; (4) home-smoked barbecue pork sandwiches; (5) steaks; and (6) pizza and the related calzone. The Valley takes its pizza seriously. There are at least 20 different styles of pizza in the Valley, all homemade and each unique.

If beer is king in the Valley, then food is queen. Take, for example, Knuckleheads, a bar in Swoyersville. We met a friend there on a Tuesday evening, and within an hour, we were buddies with everyone in the bar, including an entire bowling team—and we were buying rounds for each other. A rollicking good time. It's not our usual bar, as it served only the national mass-market stuff, the local lager (*Yuengling Lager*), and "Steg" (*Stegmaier Lager*). But the food! Homemade by Grandma in the back, the menu changes according to her whim. On the weekend, she cooked up potato pancakes, homemade clam chowder, hand-filled pierogies, and lasagna.

One current favorite watering hole is the Anthracite Cafe in the Parsons section of Wilkes-Barre. Located in a former VFW lodge and named for the large chunks of shiny coal on display behind the bar, it has a fantastic chef, and all food is prepared from scratch in their own kitchen. There are nightly specials—we love the Seafood Wednesdays. The draft list is exceptional, and the bar often hosts a "tap takeover" to showcase a regional brewery. We recently met the crew from Susquehanna Brewing Co., got a couple of free beer glasses, and tasted their offerings. We were impressed by their *6th Generation Stock Ale*—a nice session beer, reminiscent of an English bitter.

Mike, the owner of the Anthracite Cafe, is often seated at the bar and ready to tell his fish tales; he closes the cafe for a week every July to go fishing. He is much more knowledgeable about beer than I am, and he lets me try anything on the list. I decided it was time for him to learn something about bourbons, so I brought him a bottle of *Eagle Rare* to taste. Bringing a bottle to a bartender is da equivalent of coals to Newcastle, heyna? Especially at the Anthracite Cafe!

A few of our other favorites in Wilkes-Barre are Elmer Sudds, Bart & Urby's, and Beer Boys. Sudds is a very small venue with a very large menu (we recommend the steamed clams); surprisingly, they can fit an entire band in the back for a live music show. They always have the latest release from Breaker Brewing Company on draft. B&U is near the Wilkes University campus and seems to have an intellectual spin to it, filled as it is with college professors, intense conversation, and good beer. Beer Boys is another college bar with an excellent draft list and nightly food specials.

The Arena Bar and Grill is relatively new and is located near the Mohigan Sun Arena. The entire area is the site of a former strip mine that has now been developed into malls, restaurants, and other retail businesses. The Arena has a huge draft selection; you can taste pretty much any current regionals, as well as a few imports. There are over 20 beers on draft, and there's a lively happy hour on Sunday evening. Our main complaint with Arena is that they serve beer in mugs that are fresh and warm out of the dishwasher, making for an often unpleasant contrast to a chilled draft.

Cooper's is known to many readers as the after-work bar in the TV series *The Office*, which takes place in Scranton. Yes, there really is a Cooper's, and it serves great beer and seafood.

CHAPTER 4: OUR REGIONAL BEERS: NEPA

Cooper's began after World War II as a restaurant owned by the Kupris family—who were Lithuanians and distant relatives of my husband, Rick. (I have heard that all Lithuanians in the Valley are related by a few degrees.) Kupris' changed its name to Cooper's Seafood House and opened a second branch restaurant in Pittston, in the Valley. Cooper's is noted for lobster tails.

Then there are the "tough" bars, the local workingman's bars, and biker bars.

One Saturday, Rick and I drove to West Nanticoke to visit J J Banko's, a rough-and-ready combination biker bar and yuppie foodie haven. Not long ago, they were underwater—literally—as a result of the Susquehanna River flood of 2011. It was not the first time they'd been inundated, and they reopened quickly. Their beer list is uninspired and inexpensive, but their seafood is exceptional. We were not disappointed by their crab cakes!

On the way to J J Banko's, we drove through the little town of Plymouth, where Rick pointed out that when he turned 21, he tried to stop at every bar in town for one drink. He never made it—there were 76 bars on Main Street back then. This time we counted 16 drinking establishments in a single mile. Yes, it appears dat tings haven't changed much in da Valley, heyna?

And if you want to find out more about Heyna, check out the YouTube video "Heynabonics" at http://www.youtube.com/watch?v=7sMI2jb16eo to get a better understanding of the Valley accent.

ELECTRIC CITY CRAFT BREW FEST: 2013

YourBeerNetwork.com (May 15, 2013)
with Eugene Westbrook and Annie Tasker

April is upon us, and it's time for the Second Annual Electric City Craft Brew Fest in Scranton, Pennsylvania. You may recall that I attended the First annual ECCBF in April of 2012, shortly after I moved to Wilkes-Barre. It was a great introduction to the beer culture of NEPA. The fest was a great success—and I tasted a lot of beer!

This year I had two helpers, Gene Westbrook and Annie Tasker, who are my son and his fiancée, respectively. Our agenda: to pick out a selection from our regional breweries to serve at an upcoming family event, where we expected about 50 guests. We set the following specifications: the beers could include both lagers and ales, they had to be available in bottles or cans, and the majority should be session beers (alcohol less than 5% ABV). And of course, they would have to be wonderfully tasty and pair well with food. We collected our five-ounce beer glasses and started tasting.

Our first stop was **Susquehanna Brewing Company** (SBC). This brewery is a Valley success story, since they started almost from scratch in 2012, releasing their first beer in May of that year. They now have a line of four very diverse year-round brews, all available in bottles. (There are four seasonal brews as well.) We tasted the following beers:

Goldencold Lager: This was by far the best lager at the festival, beating the local standards—*Yuengling* and *Stegmaier*—hands down. It's refreshing and great with food—and I am *not* a lager lover!

6th Generation Stock Ale: Unfortunately, this was not on tap at the festival, but it has long been my pick for a perfect session ale. At 5.5% ABV and 44 IBU, it's well-balanced.

Breaker Brewing Company is another up-and-coming brewery in the Wilkes-Barre area. They have been increasing production but are still not consistently bottling, so you have to find them on draft in the area. They have opened a highly acclaimed tasting room, which is worth visiting for the hilltop view, as well as for the beer. [Author update: since this article was published, Breaker has begun operating a brewpub and bottling some of their beers.]

CHAPTER 4: OUR REGIONAL BEERS: NEPA

Our favorites include the following:

Lunch Pail Ale is a nice, mild, clean session beer that's lightly hopped and eminently drinkable. It's a great favorite of mine and good with food.

I Love PA (I♥PA) is one of the best IPAs in the region, but it's hard to find on draft. It was one of the best IPAs I tasted at the Fest this year.

ShawneeCraft Brewing Company was the one to keep an eye on at the last festival, being a small brewpub with a commitment to quality and organic ingredients. They had a lot of potential. At the time, they did not distribute outside their brewpub, but this year, I have seen them on draft at several bars. At the brewfest, I tasted their *Session Porter* and was very taken with it. On Nitro tap (meaning the CO_2 has been replaced with nitrogen and the beer is thus served without carbonation), it is more Guinness than *Guinness* itself! It's a great beer that I hope to see it in my neighborhood pubs soon.

3 Guys & A Beer'd Brewing Company has a relatively low production of consistently high-quality beers with unusual names. Among the beers we tried were the following:

Ladder Dive Rye IPA was my "best of show" last year. It tastes as good this year as it did last year.

Carbon D'Alien is a pale ale session beer, at 5.5% ABV, with a good head and perfect hop. The name refers to a UFO encounter on November 9, 1974, when a small group of teenage boys reported seeing a glowing unidentified flying object crash into a pond near the southern edge of Carbondale, Pennsylvania. I'm not sure of the connection between the event and the brewery, but I can speculate.

Victory Brewing Company, located near Philadelphia, previewed two of their summer beers. One caught our eye (and palate). *Swing Session Saison* is a light summer beer with added grains (rye, oats, and wheat). Not very hoppy, it features orange and lemon flavors, and at 4.5% ABV, you can drink it all afternoon. This was Annie's pick of the show.

TO YOUR HEALTH!

Surprise! **Old Forge** has a beer—sort of. Old Forge is a town noted for the best pizza in the country (and probably the most pizzerias on a single stretch of Main Street), and for whatever reason, a brewpub in Danville decided to start brewing beers under the **Old Forge Brewing Company** name. Their beers are surprisingly good, and I was even more surprised to find that they produce their beer in cans, rather than in bottles—a growing niche market, which I'm glad they're addressing. Their beers hold up beautifully in cans. We tasted the following:

Overbite IPA, at 7.5% ABV, is a very acceptable Pennsylvania-style IPA. It's nicely balanced but could use a bit more aroma (more dry hopping).

T-Rail Pale Ale, at 5.3% ABV, is a very drinkable session beer, well-hopped and true to style.

Flying Fish Brewing Co. is a favorite local New Jersey brewery, and I have enjoyed everything they produce. I am particularly fond of their *Hopfish IPA*. They are now creating a line of beers named for exits on the New Jersey Turnpike. We tasted two of them: *Exit 16* is an 8% ABV IPA made with wild rice. It is beautifully hopped to 62 IBUs with Citra, Columbus, Centennial, Simcoe, and Chinook; and it is then dry-hopped with Chinook and Citra hops to give it an elegant nose. It was a real knockout and Eugene's pick of the show.

Exit 4 is a Belgian Style tripel at 10.2% ABV, and it was my husband's pick for the Fest.

At this point, it was time to stop. So many beers, so little time, and so early in the day.

OUR FINAL PICKS

Our picks for our family dinner are as follows. They're all available in cans or bottles, are produced locally, and are mostly session beers:

SBC *Goldencold Lager*
SBC *6th Generation Stock Ale*

CHAPTER 4: OUR REGIONAL BEERS: NEPA

Victory *Swing Session Saison*
Old Forge *T-Rail Pale Ale*
Flying Fish *Exit 16 IPA*

A few comments about the Electric City Craft Brew Fest. The biggest change this year was the availability of free food, which is a wonderful idea, especially if you expect to start drinking at noon. The crowds were bigger this year, and I was glad that I purchased VIP tickets, which allowed us early entry with a smaller group of tasters. The festival was larger this year, expanding to all four floors and the mezzanine of the Scranton Cultural Center, and it featured over 60 beer selections from over 30 brewers.

Unfortunately, not all of the showcased beers were what I would call "craft beer," since much of the space was occupied by the larger distributors, who included some mass-market beers in their offerings. On the other hand, if that's what it takes to get people into the venue and introduce more of them to good craft beers, then I am in favor. I look forward to next year's event.

THE BEST SUMMER BEER YOU'LL NEVER TASTE—BREAKER BREWING COMPANY

YourBeerNetwork.com (July 23, 2013)

I have a microbrewery in my neighborhood. I am blessed—in fact, I am twice blessed, because not only is it so close to home, but it is also on the former site of St. Joseph's Monastery. And who can brew beer better than monks?

There are at least five purported patron saints of brewing—that's important in a Catholic town like Wilkes-Barre—but the only one with credentials is a monk: St. Arnold of Soissons (ca. 1040–1087 CE), who was himself a brewer and is depicted with a bishop's miter and a mash rake. Although monks did not invent beer, they were responsible for improving the brewing process and introducing hops. Most monasteries felt obligated to keep their regions well supplied with beer—which in medieval times was much safer to drink than was the local water supply.

In the same tradition, it is wonderful to have a brewery in a nearby (former) monastery to keep our region well supplied with beer. Breaker is an easy stop on my way home from work to pick up a growler or two. The tasting room is open three evenings a week for free-flowing beer, conversation, and an occasional snack brought in by a local patron. You will usually find one of the brewer/owners, Chris Miller or Mark Lehman, chatting with the visitors and showing off the brews. Chris and Mark's enthusiasm is contagious. They love brewing, started the enterprise as home brewers in their garage, and are rightly proud of their brewery and the beers they make.

Breaker's new brewery and tasting room is located along a beautiful and steep drive, Laurel Run. This historic road, which is locally known as Giant's Despair, is the site of many crashes. The road is the site of a yearly summer car race, the Giant's Despair Hillclimb, which has been going on since the early 1900s. It is a dramatic setting overlooking the Wyoming Valley. You can see the sites of many former anthracite coal mines, some of which are only a few miles from the brewery, which explains the brewery's name and logo.

A *breaker* is a coal-processing plant that is used for breaking up and sorting raw coal ore brought up from the deep underground mines. Although Wyoming Valley's history dates back to prerevolutionary times, it was the European immigrants that came to mine coal in the 1800s and early 1900s who brought the demand for beer. The coal mines are now closed due to an underground flood in 1959, but most locals still feel a strong connection to the miners, and that is one reason why Breaker is so well loved. (The other reason is the good brew.)

Most everyone from around here is only one or two degrees removed from mining. My husband, Rick, had two Lithuanian grandfathers who were miners. One, Grandpa Rakauskas, worked at the Stanton Colliery, which was only a few miles from where the tasting room is today. Grandpa Gober worked across

CHAPTER 4: OUR REGIONAL BEERS: NEPA

Enjoying a fresh draft with the brewer-owners Chris Miller and Mark Lehman, at the Breaker Brewery Tasting Room.

the river at the Harry E. Colliery, just a couple of blocks up the hill from the house he shared with his family. Rick remembers how Gober would walk home carrying his empty lunch pail, tired and thirsty at the end of a long day, stopping at Antanaitas's tavern along the way to fill up the pail with beer to drink at home.

Breaker pays homage to the anthracite coal miners who lived and worked in the area. The tasting room is filled with miner's memorabilia, including miner's lamps, lunch pails, and old-time photos of the area and the miners. It is a veritable history museum, a delight for the local coal aficionados. And of course, the beer names memorialize the miners and their lives.

Lunch Pail Ale is the flagship. It is American pale ale, and it's currently my go-to beer in local bars. At 5.0% ABV, it's incredibly drinkable, with a beautiful amber color, good malt flavor from Munich malts, and a highly hopped (45 IBU) but balanced flavor. It uses mostly West Coast hops—Columbus, Cascade, and Nugget. It has a great aroma, thanks to dry-hopping. Every time I drink it, I think of Grandpa Gober and his lunch pail, through in reality, he probably drank a lighter, lower-alcohol beer—possibly a pale ale or, more likely, *Gibbons Lager*, which was well loved but is now defunct.

Goldies Blonde Ale is probably closer to what Grandpa Gober drank. It's an easy-drinking session beer, at 4.5% ABV, with only a smattering of hops (12 IBU), leaving a distinctive clove-and-banana finish. Goldie's was an establishment in downtown Wilkes-Barre where local coal miners would unwind with beer, food, and "merriment." I'm still not sure what "merriment" is, but it might have involved Goldie. Last week I tried *Goldies Extra Blonde Ale*, which is the same recipe but brewed with twice the malt, resulting in a 7% ABV beer. Excellent! It is much better than regular *Goldies*, and it has much more merriment.

A few weeks ago, I stopped in at Breaker's tasting room to see what was on tap and to catch up with the brewers. The draft list contained their standards, which include a stout and several IPAs, all very good—and incidentally, they make an outstanding black IPA, *Black Diamond*. There was a new addition, *5 Whistle Watermelon Wheat*. If you are a regular reader, you probably know that I'm not a big fan of wheat beers or summer fruit beers, and I am especially skeptical of beers that feature "weird" ingredients.

I was not prepared for this beer, which was an exceptional summer ale. This beer used their standard *5 Whistle Wheat* beer as a base, with added watermelon juice for flavoring. Unlike many summer beers and pumpkin ales, the fruit was not used in the fermentation process because, as Mark explained, doing it that way ended up making the beer taste like watermelon rind. But using the juice as a flavor additive worked beautifully. The beer is crisp, cold, and thirst quenching, watermelony but not too sweet. I took a growler along to a picnic that evening, and it went quickly. This is the best summer beer I have ever tasted. I hope they feature it again next summer.

CHAPTER 4: OUR REGIONAL BEERS: NEPA

I returned a few weeks later for more, but sadly, the *5 Whistle Watermelon Wheat* was all gone. Instead, I was handed a draft of another summer wheat beer, this one flavored with lemongrass—*Laurel Line Lemongrass Ale*. The ale is named for an interurban light rail line that connected Scranton and Wilkes-Barre—The Laurel Line, a.k.a. The Lackawanna and Wyoming Valley Railroad. *Laurel Line* is a fun beer to drink because it tastes like lemonade. It's very similar to a traditional shandy, which in England is a beer mix of 50% English ale and 50% lemon soda.

I was initially skeptical because the only other lemongrass beer I had ever tasted was *Monkey Knife Fight*, at Nodding Head Brewery in Philadelphia. I did not care for *Monkey* at all, in part due to its confusing and unpleasant flavor mix, which includes ginger, spice, and lemongrass. *Monkey* has its followers, but I am not one of them. But *Laurel Line* has one flavor—lemon—and it's done correctly.

Unfortunately, most of my readers will never get a chance to taste these wonderful beers because Breaker is a microbrewery, which means its annual production is small (fewer than 15,000 barrels, by definition of the American Brewers Association). In general, the smaller and more hands-on the brewery, the better the beer—but there is less of it.

Like most micros, Breaker doesn't bottle, and Mark and Chris do most of their own distribution. They can barely make enough to keep up with demand. They brew in three-barrel batches (1 beer barrel = 31 gallons) and often hit gridlock, waiting for the brew to finish so they can move in another beer. I was pleased to hear that they are adding more tank capacity. This will double their output, so the beer will soon be flowing more freely. Along with this, they're going to expand their tasting room into a full-time brewpub, serving food and drink.

In the meantime, I'm happy to enjoy the small pours at the tasting room, take home the occasional growler, and seek out BBC on draft at the local saloons. I recognize that bottling is not a realistic plan for such a small enterprise, and it would probably have a negative impact on their quality or innovation if they chose to go in that direction at this time. Too many small breweries have been ruined by scaling up too fast. I'm happy to keep Breaker as *my* local "monastery," keeping our region supplied with freshly brewed beer.

This is not a plea to Breaker to scale up, expand, and start bottling—though if that happened, I would be the first in line so I could take a few cases to out-of-state friends. (I'll bring one for you, Harvey!) It is, instead, a reminder to love and support your local microbrewery. Amen.

[Author Update: As of March 2014, Breaker has expanded capacity, is operating a brewpub on site, and is bottling some of its beer.]

BEER IN THE VALLEY: ELECTRIC CITY CRAFT BREW FEST, NOVEMBER, 2013

YourBeerNetwork.com (December 9, 2013)

Craft beer is not only alive and well in NEPA—it is thriving. This is the conclusion I drew after attending the third Electric City Craft Brew Fest on Saturday, November 16, 2013.

The ECBrewfest, previously held in March in Scranton ("Electric City"), was moved to Wilkes-Barre to coincide with the November opening of a new venue—the convention center in the new hotel at the Mohegan Sun casino. This was a smart move. It brought out the crowds, who were curious to see the new venue. It also brought out some old friends, such as Carl—local bartender and proprietor of Carl's Beer Tours—who brought along about a dozen beer aficionados. The venue provided a lot more space, all on one floor—which made for a much better experience than did the historic but confusing multiroom hall in Scranton. And parking at the casino was ample and free.

There was an extensive selection of beer from craft breweries as far away as Colorado and Virginia, as well as a few big-

CHAPTER 4: OUR REGIONAL BEERS: NEPA

ger names that rightly didn't belong there but were featured by the distributors who had booths at the fest. In fact, I got into a friendly disagreement with a distributor wearing a *Budweiser* shirt, who insisted that *Budweiser* was the original craft beer!

As I have done at previous ECBrewfests (see YourBeerNetwork.com, May 13 and May 15, 2013), I limited my tasting to regional craft beers; that day, it would be all Pennsylvania beers. My tastings included some well-known local brewers: 3 Guys & A Beer'd (Carbondale, Pennsylvania), Breaker (Wilkes-Barre Township, Pennsylvania) ShawneeCraft (Shawnee on Delaware), Fegley's (Lehigh Valley), Old Forge (Danville), Stoudt's (Adamstown), Weyerbacher (Easton), Yards (Philadelphia), and Victory (Downingtown). New to the venue, and to me, were Penn Brewery (Pittsburgh), Manayunk Brewery (Philadelphia), Erie Brewing (Erie), Free Will Brewing (Perkasie), and Nimble Hill Brewing (Tunkhannock). Of these, Free Will and Nimble Hill are relatively young start-ups, while Manayunk is a well-established brewpub now distributing beer in cans.

To pace myself, I set a limit of two-and-a-half pints, spread out over three hours, with food to slow down alcohol absorption (see chapter 3, "Alcohol, Part 1: Your Brain on Beer"). That meant small pours (no more than 2.5 ounces per brewery) and a lot of pierogies.

This year, the breweries really showed off their stuff, and there was a lot to taste besides IPAs and pale ales. I was fortunate to buy one of the limited tickets to the VIP session, which gave me the opportunity to taste a number of innovative and creative limited-edition brews. I also had extra time to talk to the brewers, such as Johnny Waering ("The Guy With the Beer'd") from 3 Guys & A Beer'd Brewing Co. and John Stemler from Free Will Brewing.

The folks in NEPA have traditionally favored lagers, with *Yuengling* and *Stegmaier* having been the local standards for the last few decades. I was pleased to see that NEPA has discovered craft beers and has embraced ales and hops. Every brewery is now producing an IPA, and I'm not going to review them; they are all excellent, and every local has his own favorite.

TO YOUR HEALTH!

My current favorites are Nimble Hill's *Hop Bottom*, which uses locally grown Cascade and Centennial hops and is packed with flavor; and Breaker's perfectly hopped *Lunch Pail Ale*, which I prefer even over their excellent *I Love PA*—because at 5.5% ABV, I can drink more of it.

I confess that, for the most part, I skipped lagers at this Fest, since overall, I prefer ales (yes, I am a hophead). I made an exception for Penn Brewing, which is known for the lager-based styles; I can recommend their *Cool River Kölsch*, which is surprisingly light and easy to drink and goes well with pierogies. I also avoided the pumpkin ales—again, they're not my favorites.

Popular this year were brews using fruits and nuts. As you might expect for a November brewfest, cranberry was a popular flavor. Manayunk featured a *Schuykill Punch Raspberry Ale*, which was forgettable, at 6% ABV and only 14 IBUs. (I heard many raves about it—go figure!) Weyerbacher showed off their *Althea* double IPA, which was brewed with plums; ShawneeCraft featured a *Cranberry IPA*; and Breaker offered their *Cranberry Ginger IPA*, as well as their *Sour Pear*. More on these later.

More on these breweries:

ShawneeCraft Brewing Company is a microbrewery that I had wanted to keep an eye on at the last brewfest. Their commitment is to produce a beer that uses locally sourced, primarily organic ingredients. Keeping this goal is a challenge when scaling up, but they have succeeded and are now producing enough that I see their beer on draft even as far away as Wilkes-Barre. I was especially impressed with their *Chestnut Braun Ale*. This was an English-style brown ale made using hybrid, blight-resistant American chestnuts. The nuts gave a bitter, hop-like flavor that I found worked well with the malty brown flavor; the beer was very drinkable at 5.5% ABV.

3 Guys & A Beer'd was just getting off the ground at the last brewfest, but they have clearly established themselves. They are now producing enough to bottle and distribute regionally, though their beer is still hard to find. I liked their *Loyalty Barber*

CHAPTER 4: OUR REGIONAL BEERS: NEPA

Shop Shaving Cream Ale (5.5% ABV), a traditional-tasting cream ale. I'm not sure why we don't see more cream ales—which are easy-drinking, low-hop-style ales that go well with food, as this one does.

I talked for a while with John Stemler, cofounder and brewmaster of **Free Will Brewing Company** in Perkasie, a very small town in Bucks County, Pennsylvania. The brewery has tremendous potential, and they are expanding rapidly and are starting to bottle. Their notable beers include these two:

Alexander: This was a tart saison, brewed with *Brettannomyces* yeast, aged on sour Montmorency cherries, and conditioned on American oak, at 6.10% ABV. I was impressed, but I had to agree with John that it will probably be even better when it has had a chance to bottle-condition for another year.

C.O.B. stands for "Coffee Oatmeal Brown." This is an imperial-style English brown ale that is aged on coffee. It is very dense in flavor, malty, and sweet, and the coffee taste comes through nicely. 8.3% ABV.

Breaker Brewing Company, my local microbrewery (see "The Best Summer Beer You'll Never Taste"), was well represented at the brewfest. In addition to their standard ales, IPAs, and porters, they showcased three of their more creative efforts: *Sour Ale, Cranberry Ginger Goldies,* and *Sour Pear.* Of these, the most interesting were the sours, which were brewed in the old style, using wild yeast with open brewing.

The *Sour Ale* itself was palatable but one-dimensional; the *Sour Pear* included the addition of fresh pear. This beer was quite remarkable and unlike anything I had tasted before. I expected a Belgian-style lambic, but it was more reminiscent of a fresh cider. *The Cranberry Ginger Goldies* was a solid, drinkable fruit beer using their *Goldies Blonde Ale* as a base. The ginger flavor is subtle but noticeable, making this a good holiday selection that's especially suitable for Thanksgiving.

There were some negatives to the brewfest venue, one of which was the fact that the beer had to be poured by Mohegan Sun bartenders instead of the brewery staff. As a result, the brewery staff would wander off, so they were not around to answer questions and promote their beer. Also, the casino bartenders were often not knowledgeable about the brews they were pouring.

Another disappointment was the food. At the Cultural Center venue, there had been a variety of food to sample or purchase from several Scranton-based restaurants. Here, the only options were bar food—pretzels, nachos, wings, pierogies, popcorn, and hot dogs. They were nice for a snack but a bit too heavy after a couple of hours of trying to balance alcohol intake with light food during the VIP-session noon hour. I would have appreciated something a bit healthier or more satisfying for lunch—such as sandwiches, soup, or salad.

Finally: too many beers, too little time. If you were a serious taster, there was no time at all to attend the beer-school seminars on Belgian beers and United Kingdom ales. I would have loved to come back and taste the beers that I missed and catch the seminars. A note to the organizers: *Please* make this a two-day event!

Below are my beer picks for the November 2013 Electric City Craft Brew Fest:

1. **IPA**
   No favorites. All good.

2. **Fruit-based beer**
   Breaker's *Sour Pear*
   Breaker's *Cranberry Ginger Goldies*
   Weyerbacher's *Althea*

3. **Sour or Belgian-style**
   Free Will's *Alexander*
   Breaker's *Sour Pear*

4. **Dark beer**
   Susquehanna Brewing Co.'s *Pils Noir*
   ShawneeCraft's *Chestnut Braun Ale*
   Free Will's *C.O.B*

CHAPTER 4: OUR REGIONAL BEERS: NEPA

5. **Oktoberfest or malty-style**
   Erie's *Railbender Ale*
   Susquehanna Brewing Co.'s *Toboggan Chocolate Doppelbock*

6. **Craziest out-in-left-field beer—and why**
   Victory Brewing Company's *Red Thunder* (8.5%). This one was aged in oak wine barrels, with whiskey added. Crazy, but it works.

   Stoudt's *The Big Nasty* (10.5% ABV and 160 IBU). I can't taste all the hops, but it has the most delightfully lingering finish I have ever found in a beer.

Carol enjoying a Harpoon IPA *with fried clams in Boston.*

CHAPTER 5

REGIONAL BEERS FROM OTHER AREAS

Like NEPA, every region has its own beer styles, bar culture, and local breweries. I enjoy travel, and when I visit an area that is new to me, I try to get a sense of the beer *terroir*.

The following articles showcase the variety of craft beer that I have experienced on these travels, from East Coast to West, and the venues in which they are enjoyed.

BOSTON IS A GREAT BEER CITY: A.K.A. FORGET SAM ADAMS

YourBeerNetwork.com (February 4, 2011)

Boston is the Mecca of Western Medicine. It is the home of Harvard Medical School—the premier institution of its kind in the world—as well as of two other med schools, Tufts and Boston University. Cambridge, just across the river, is a center of biotechnology research and the pharmaceutical industry, where new drugs are discovered, analyzed, tested, and produced daily. MIT, also in Cambridge, is a powerhouse of science, learning, and entrepreneurs.

What does this have to do with beer? Lots. Boston has a disproportionate share of people under age 40 who are highly intelligent; have advanced degrees in biology, medicine, or engineering; and drink beer. Lots of beer. They demand good beer to go along with the variety of food that is available in Boston, which tends toward remarkably fresh fish and shellfish, vegetarian food, and a variety of ethnic delights—including Portuguese, Irish, Vietnamese, Thai, Japanese, Russian, and Polish food, among others.

What pairs best with seafood, vegetarian food, and spicy ethnic food? Why, IPAs, of course! Bostonians prefer IPAs that have complex hops but are only moderately bitter and are lower in alcohol than, say, San Diego ales. These IPAs are more closely related to true English IPAs, rather than to their higher-alcohol and hoppier West Coast cousins.

Though Boston has only a few breweries of its own, it is well positioned to take advantage of the many East Coast microbreweries noted for this style of beer, including Victory, Dogfish Head, Ipswich, and Boston's own Harpoon.

During a recent trip to Boston over the New Year's holiday (2011), I was delighted to see that most restaurants had an excellent draft list—and some even suggested pairings. The thirty-somethings of Boston were more likely to be found with a glass of ale than with a martini or wine. In fact, there are considerably more beer bars in Boston than in most other cities twice its size. (I define a beer bar as having 10 or more taps, with a selection of drafts from independent brewers.)

Why are the bar and restaurant draft lists in Boston so good compared to, say, Chicago, where you are likely to be offered only *Bud Light* or *Miller* on draft? The answer is supply and demand. As my colleague Paul Ciminero—former wine distributor and staff writer for YourBeerNetwork—explains, it's all about the beer distributorships, which have to move a certain number of the large mass-markets beers.

In Chicago, the bars and restaurants are expected to serve the mass-market stuff, and that's all the patrons expect. In Boston, there is such a demand from the bars and restaurants that they also provide the good stuff. This is something you hopheads should keep in mind: keep drinking those microbrews and

CHAPTER 5: REGIONAL BEERS FROM OTHER AREAS

keep requesting them at your local watering hole. Don't settle for *Bud Light*.

What I drank in Boston:

1. **At the airport.**

   The minute I stepped off the plane at Logan Airport, I walked over to Legal Sea Foods and ordered a fried clam roll, washed down with a large draft of *Harpoon IPA*. Yes, in the airport! In my opinion, *Harpoon IPA* is the perfect match for seafood. At 5.9% ABV, it contains substantial amounts of Northern Cascade hops, which are floral but not overly bitter, with a touch of Apollo hops to add strength.

2. **At the New Year's Day dinner party** with some young professionals and two old geezers (my spouse and me).

   Everyone brought beer to pair with vegetarian fare and birthday cake. What did they bring?

   With starters: Dogfish Head's *60 Minute IPA*, a much-loved East Coast IPA brewed in Delaware, with Northwest hops added continuously over 60 minutes. At 6.0% ABV, it's a good session beer to start the evening.

   With the main course: *Sierra Nevada Celebration Ale, 2010*. This is a unique beer made with fresh hops, primarily Cascade and Centennial, that impart a fresher, grassy flavor. At 6.8% ABV, it pairs perfectly with vegetarian fare.

   With homemade chocolate cake: Dogfish Head's *Raison D'Etre*, a spicy, hoppy barley wine (8.0% ABV) made with beet sugar and Belgian yeast.

3. **At Bukowski's.**

   There are quite a few good beer bars in the Boston area, including the world-renowned Sunset Grill & Tap (112 taps!), the Publick House (31 taps), and the Bukowski Tavern (30 taps). So much beer, so little time! Since we could visit only one, we

TO YOUR HEALTH!

went to Bukowski's. The original Bukowski's is a punk bar in a downtown Boston parking garage. We prefer their other site, in Cambridge, Massachusetts, which was within staggering distance of our old house.

Bukowski's has recently expanded their draft list, and they serve up an ever-changing selection of regional microbrews and a few imports. They are also noted for a large selection of bottled beers, their proverbial "99 bottles of beer on the wall," which is represented on a roulette-like wheel. If you can't make up your mind, spin the bottle.

We visited Bukowski's with our friend Carly, who was an associate producer for NPR's *Car Talk*, also a Boston institution. We tasted quite a few drafts, and here are two at the extreme ends of the spectrum:

Black Perle Dark IPA, from RJ Rockers (South Carolina), is a remarkably dark IPA, made with a huge amount of roasted malt, giving it 9.5% ABV. It is "octo-hopped" with the German Perle hop.

Blanche de Bruxelles, from Brasserie Lefèbrve, is an unfiltered white beer from Belgium containing only 4.5% ABV. It is made with 40% wheat, flavored with orange peel and coriander. It's a very palatable session beer, but perhaps it's more suited to a summer afternoon than a snowy January day.

4. **At the Harpoon Brewery.**

    If you visit only one brewery in Boston, this is the one. Visit on a weekday afternoon at 4:00 p.m. and you can skip the tedious tour and go right to the tasting. Harpoon generously lets you taste any of their drafts as many times as you like, in 3-ounce portions. Their 12 taps had Harpoon standards, including their IPA, a Belgian pale ale (like *Leffe Blonde*), several UFO beers (unfiltered wheat beer, with fruit flavors) a surprisingly palatable Harpoon cider, and two small-batch "100-barrel brews."

CHAPTER 5: REGIONAL BEERS FROM OTHER AREAS

The 100-barrel brews are brewers' experiments. Of the two 100-barrel brews, we loved the *Leviathan*, a huge barley wine with 10% ABV; at 120 bittering units, that's about three times the IBU of a typical IPA. More interesting but less drinkable was the *Pilgrim Ale*, which attempted to reproduce a typical beer made in colonial America. This low-alcohol brew was flavored with sage, since hops were not in cultivation in the U.S. during colonial times.

5. **With lobster, in Maine.**

    Nothing! I was the designated driver for our drive up to L.L. Bean in Rockport, Maine, to catch the holiday sales—so no beer for me. We ended our day with a fabulous dinner of fresh, local lobster. If I'd had a drink with my lobster, it would have been a good East Coast IPA—*Ipswich Ale* or an IPA from Allagash Brewing Company or Shipyard Brewing Company.

OUR LOCAL BARS: OFF THE BEATEN PATH

YourBeerNetwork.com (August 15, 2011)

It's fun to discover a good bar in an out-of-the-way place. Quaint, charming, and great to visit once. But what if you actually have to live off the beaten path? How in the world do you find a good place for a beer?

    Let me explain. When I took a job as a doctor in Goshen, Indiana, I was looking forward to living in a quiet rural community... a town surrounded by farms and orchards... where I could get local produce and farm-raised beef... a town that values family and church... where restaurants are closed on Sunday ... where I could hear the clip-clop of Amish buggies.

    Then ... OMG! I'm 150 miles from Chicago! What am I going to do? Where am I going to find a place to get a good draft beer? Worse yet, will I have to drink at home?

TO YOUR HEALTH!

The search began for a suitable bar. Requirements were as follows: good beer on draft, open late, good food, interesting patrons to chat with, and good bartenders who remember your name. In other words, beer and ambiance. And oh, it had to be close to home.

I won't tell you about all the sad, smoke-filled joints we visited. "Irish" pubs without even *Guinness* on draft. Bars with no taps, only bottles. Lousy pizza and thin beer, with cigarette smoke everywhere. Wonderful Mexican restaurants with home cooking and Mexican draft beers, but which closed at 9:00 p.m. Finally, we narrowed it down to two bars: Constant Spring and the Landmark. Here's the lowdown:

1. **Constant Spring** does everything right, and it could hold its own against any good Chicago pub. CS has been open for five years, and it was started by proprietors Mark and Jason, graduates of Goshen College. Goshen College is a conservative Mennonite institution, where drinking is not as widespread as it is in other colleges. Jason and Mark had no experience managing either restaurants or bars, but they knew what they wanted and created it in Goshen, Indiana.

    First of all, CS is clean, healthy, youthful, organic, and the only smoke-free bar in Goshen. The draft list is outstanding, with a changing selection of regional and national microbrews and a few imports. You can always find *Bell's Two Hearted Ale* on draft and always something from Left Hand Brewing Company and Three Floyds Brewing. PBR is on draft, but there's no Bud. The food is very good for a bar, stressing local produce and organic ingredients—even in the burgers.

    Jason and Mark know me by name, as do most of the bartenders. The ambiance is first-rate: free popcorn, trivia night on Tuesdays, karaoke on Wednesdays, and occasional live rock on Fridays. Best of all, there's great conversation with whoever is sitting next to you at the bar. The most interesting people hang at CS, from college students to old

CHAPTER 5: REGIONAL BEERS FROM OTHER AREAS

geezers, from farmers to laborers to artists—and all with a story to tell.

Downside: CS is not open on Sundays, and the kitchen closes at 10:00 p.m.

2. **Landmark Bar & Grill** is a short five miles from Goshen in New Paris—a town which is neither New nor Paris. There's little industry left in town, and folks don't have much to spend. This has probably been the case since the bar opened, which I'm guessing was in the 1920s—before Prohibition? It certainly *is* a landmark. By the look of the old pictures on the wall, it has changed little since then.

   The Landmark is everything Constant Spring is not. Smoking is permitted. The draft beer list has only the big brands (e.g., *Miller* and *Bud Light*), though there is an acceptable selection of bottled beers. The bartenders don't know us. The bar has no website, though it is on Facebook. The food is, well, fried—fried chicken, fish, pork chops, and gizzards (yes, gizzards). What it lacks in fresh, organic ingredients it makes up for in cheap, plentiful portions.

   Ambiance? Live music tends toward country and western. There are poker nights and karaoke nights. The clientele are older, bearded, or bikers. The grease monkeys and stockers from New Paris Speedway are frequent guests and rave about the food. Landmark doesn't pretend to be a dive bar—it is a dive bar. Bar fights break out (or so I'm told). But if you get to the Saturday night prime rib special before 5:00 p.m., you'll see families and a table or two of oldsters from the local retirement communities.

   And that's why we like Landmark so much. It feels so homey. It is the only gathering place in a relatively poor town, where everyone tolerates everyone else. It has the feel of an old-time saloon, down to the swinging doors. It doesn't meet our sophisticated "beer and ambiance" criteria above, but it's a great place to go. You can always get a beer and a meal, cheap, and you'll always feel welcome.

TO YOUR HEALTH!

VIGNETTES FROM OUR FAVORITE BARS

Constant Spring

- Two ministers walked into the bar (CS). Rick asked the first one if he believed in God. Three beers later, at the end of the night, he still was not sure about the answer.
- We won the couples' trivia night one Tuesday and won a free beer.
- We saw Pete Best (he's the fifth Beatle) and his band, live at the bar.

Landmark

- We spent New Year's Eve at Landmark in 2010. We didn't know a soul, but we danced the night away to a country and western band.
- I often run into my cancer patients, who come early for dinner and bridge.
- The first—and last—time we tried the fried chicken gizzards, they were hard as rocks and unchewable.

Sadly, my stay in Goshen is over, and I'll be leaving in the fall. But we'll be back to Constant Spring and Landmark whenever we can.

TWO GUYS WALK INTO A BAR AND ASK TO SEE THE DRAFT LIST ...A JOKE? READ ON.

YourBeerNetwork.com (September 18, 2012)

Recently, on a trip to Chicago, Rick and I walked into the Hopleaf. Long one of our favorite beer bars, it has become nationally recog-

CHAPTER 5: REGIONAL BEERS FROM OTHER AREAS

nized for its outstanding Belgian draft selection. For a while, this tavern was virtually inaccessible due to its popularity and resultant overcrowding, but now—thanks to its recent expansion—it is possible to walk in, find a seat at the bar, ask for the draft list, and have a bartender's attention when needed.

Take it from me, Chicago is an excellent beer town. With a number of superb beer bars and gastropubs, and now an increasing number of local microbreweries, Chicago is developing a regional style that is competitive with the best of San Diego or Colorado.

The bartender and I compared notes on our home brewing. He was setting up a batch of Baltic porter, and I was setting up an English bitter and my signature IPA. All are flavorful, traditional, easy-drinking beers. Then I proceeded to scan the draft list and place my order.

The front page of the menu features Belgians, from brewers like De Koninck, Chimay, and Bosteels. Classic and delicious, any pick would be good. Then I turned the menu over to the U.S. craft beers. I was looking forward to picking a new draft from among the latest releases from my favorite Midwestern breweries, and....

OMG! What's with the bizarre ingredients and over-the-top hops? Or the pair-up of local and distant breweries and of American and European brew styles that were never meant to go together? Is there anything I can trust to taste good? What's going on here?

Here are some examples copied verbatim from the beer menu:

5 Grass (Five Rabbit, Chicago)

5 Grass, a symbol of life in Aztec mythology. Refreshing yet substantial, pale in color & nicely hoppy. Smooth clean malt flavors; unique, complex nose. Meant to invoke the desert's brisk, clean aroma, it makes use of 3 unique hop varieties & some carefully chosen herbs and spices, including juniper, sage & Tasmanian pepperberry, among others—to give a beautiful outdoorsy scent. 6.2%

TO YOUR HEALTH!

Fiat Lux (Brooklyn, New York)

Draft-only release brewed with Canadian & American 2-row malts and American Madsen unmalted white winter wheat: Cascade, Chinook, Columbus, Centennial & Perle hops; and Levure Belgique yeast with the addition of lime peel and coriander. Super refreshing. 6.1%

Diversey & Lill(e) (Two Brothers, Illinois, and Castelain, France)

The first-ever collaborative beer between America & France and they certainly did it right. Dry-hopped Biere de Garde superbly balanced between hops and sweet caramel malty flavors. 6.5%

Wookey Jack (Firestone Walker, Paso Robles, California)

Black rye IPA. Rich dark malts & spicy rye careen into bold citrus-laden hops, creating a new dimension in IPA flavor. Left unfiltered & unrefined to retain all of its texture and character. 60 IBUs. 8.3%

Super IPA (New Belgium/Alpine Brewing, Fort Collins, Colorado and San Diego, California)

Alpine might be small, but their brewing chops are mighty. New Belgium teamed up with them to create this tripel dry-hopped imperial IPA bursting with Columbus, Amarillo, Centennial & Simcoe hops. Consider yourself lucky to get an Alpine beer outside of San Diego. 9%

Collaboration: ***Special Belge*** (DuPont, Belgium and Iron Hill, Pennsylvania)

Brasserie DuPont's first collaboration in its 166-year history! With Pennsylvania's Iron Hill, they've created a sessionable, yet complex, Belgian blonde ale with subtle hints of peat-smoked malt. 6.8%

MCsaison (Flossmoor Station & City Provisions Flossmoor Illinois, Chicago Illinois)

CHAPTER 5: REGIONAL BEERS FROM OTHER AREAS

The latest creation by City Provisions' Cleetus Friedman, brewed by Flossmoor Station. Saison-style beer brewed with strawberries & rhubarb, which are very subtle. The alcohol is deceptively unnoticeable. Very smooth & refreshing. 8.1%

Homo Sapient Trip Raspberry (Dark Horse, Marshall, Michigan)

A strong "one off" that will be around this month (September) only. A Belgian-style raspberry trippel w/ hibiscus & fresh raspberries, based on their regular Sapient Trip Ale. Mild fruity tartness & faint aroma of the hibiscus flower. 9.5%

Enough. OK, I can understand the appeal of fresh fruit in midseason—who can resist a blueberry ale or a peach seasonal wheat beer? And sure, pumpkin ales are as American as apple pie during the fall harvest. But rhubarb? Juniper berries? Hibiscus?

Barrel-aged beers—all right, they're a passing fad. Sometimes, they're exceptional when a good beer goes into superb Kentucky bourbon barrels—but usually, the beer was better before the aging. Extra-black IPAs? Makes no sense to me. Black malts (actually dark roasted/burnt malted barley) have been used to add color to English porters since they were first developed. They were known to work best in lightly hopped beers (e.g. *Guinness*) and are always used sparingly; otherwise, the result is an unpleasant ashy flavor, which is frankly bitter when overhopped.

I don't understand this fascination with adding more and more hops or using herbal flavorings that were abandoned after hops were widely adopted in the 16th century. Or taking a perfectly good European brew style and reinterpreting it to utilize American ingredients. To paraphrase a quote attributed to George Bernard Shaw (in which he compared women authors to dogs that could walk on two legs), it's not that they can brew it well, but that they can brew it at all.

I'm not against brewers experimenting, because that is the only way progress can be made. But please, if you're a brewer, serve it in your home brewpub, get some feedback, and don't charge me $8.50 a pint at my high-end beer bar.

Beer should taste *good*, not *interesting*!

What does this mean to the average beer drinker? First, it means you can't trust the latest release from your favorite brewery. You will have to read the descriptions, make a few guesses, and then talk to the bartender. Of course, he/she is not likely to tell you that a beer is undrinkable but will instead suggest "something you might like more." In a good beer bar, you will be given a taste of your picks so you can choose among them. But that takes time and effort when you're thirsty! Or just forget it; go to the front page and pick one of your old favorites or a Belgian import—and skip the strange brews.

Back to the Hopleaf. Our solution? Rick ordered an old standby. I read the lists, tasted, and compared. I tasted the *Diversey and Lill(e)* from the Two Brothers/Castelain collaboration (see above), comparing their dry-hopped Castelain *Biere de Garde* to the original. No question—the beer was better in its original form; it was not improved by dry hopping. What were they thinking?

Brewers, I'll give you the benefit of the doubt. I'll chalk this up to ennui. Perhaps you are just getting tired of producing the same-old delightful, hoppy, end-of-season beers—the ones I really like to drink—and want to make something new. I expect this phase will pass with the season. So be it. I never thought I would be looking forward to the fall beers—pumpkin ales and Oktoberfest knockoffs.

SUNLESS IN SEATTLE: EXPLORING THE PACIFIC NORTHWEST IN SEARCH OF THE ELUSIVE...

YourBeerNetwork.com (November 20, 2013)

... elusive (1) Yeti (Bigfoot), (2) glimpse of Mt. Rainier, and (3) exceptional beer.

CHAPTER 5: REGIONAL BEERS FROM OTHER AREAS

Carol enjoying oysters and Pike Pale Ale *in Seattle, Washington.*

I will elaborate. I had a business trip to Seattle in October, so I asked Rick to come along to give me a hand with some beer tasting after hours. After all, Washington State has 194 breweries, more than any other state except California.

It was, of course, raining continuously, so we did not have any spectacular views of Mt. Rainier, which appears in the background in most travelogues of this friendly, casual town. Though we didn't get to visit any breweries because I had to spend my days at the conference in a downtown hotel, we made it up after hours, searching for our exceptional beer.

In general, hotel bars don't have extensive beer selections, but I was pleasantly surprised to find ours had a good selection of regional craft beers. In fact, this was true for most restaurants and bars we visited, so we didn't have to go far to get a good sampling of local Seattle brews. All we had to do was eat our way through the town, which we proceeded to do.

You could start at the Pike Place Market, near my hotel. It has food stalls, restaurants, and its own brewery. Tourist trap? Yes. Authentic? Absolutely. That's me in the picture, eating local oysters paired with a Pike IPA. A perfect pair—me and oysters, that is.

Seattle's cuisine is known for exceptionally fresh seafood, smoked salmon, handcrafted cheese, and fresh produce—all of which pair remarkably well with IPAs. And that pretty much sums it up. In Seattle, they drink IPAs. On occasion you will see a double IPA or sometimes a lighter IPA masquerading as a pale ale.

Every beer we tasted was hoppier than its Midwest or East Coast cousin, no doubt because Washington is such a hop-conscious state. (The Yakima Valley in Washington State produces more than 75 percent of the hops used for brewing in the United States!) Yet we found that most beers contained well-flavored hop mixtures and were generously dry-hopped with good aroma. With all this excellent beer, it was difficult to pick out one that stood head and shoulders above the rest.

Continuing our quest, we made our way to the Tap House Grill, a beer bar that I would recommend to every YBN reader as a place you must go before you die. The Tap House has 160 beers on draft, with the taps in a beautiful, curving array that is a delight to behold! How do they manage to store and serve 160 draft beers? Our bartender, Raul, was kind enough to take us to the back to show off the keg room, with row upon row of fresh kegs. Among the good local beers we enjoyed here were *Hopchops IPA* from North Sound Brewing Co., *Immortal*

CHAPTER 5: REGIONAL BEERS FROM OTHER AREAS

IPA from Elysian Brewing, and *Lucille IPA* from Georgetown Brewing Company.

Lucille stands out as the hoppiest among hoppy beers, with an IBU of 85! The brewers threw in the kitchen sink on this one, as the hop mix includes Columbus, Centennial, Amarillo, Simcoe, and Cascade. The name *Lucille*? As the brewery notes state, "Anything so innocent and built like that just gotta be named Lucille" (as quoted from the film *Cool Hand Luke*). It's certainly a memorable beer and very enjoyable—but not the exceptional beer I was seeking.

With a draft list like the Tap House's, Rick and I found we couldn't resist the opportunity to sample Belgian beers on draft. So we shared samples of the following: *Duchesse de Bourgogne, Kwak, Chimay Trappiste* (white), *La Chouffe, St. Bernardus Abt 12, La Caracole Nostradamus,* and *Bornem Dubbel.* The *Bornem Dubbel* was new to me, and I have to admit that I've tasted much better Belgian ales; the others were excellent beers.

We continued our quest along the Pacific coast to Vancouver. It was still raining, and there was still no sighting of Bigfoot, no view of Mt. Rainier, and no beer rated as "exceptional." That's 0 for 0 on our quest.

Vancouver is only 120 miles from Seattle, and it has a lot in common with its U.S. neighbor—including rain, mountains, seafood, and salmon. In addition, Vancouver has excellent totem poles and outstanding Chinese food, with the latter due to its large and growing Hong Kong immigrant population.

We had a great time during our short stay in this cosmopolitan town. The traffic is awful, but the city has a lot to offer: great culture and good restaurants, all in a dramatic location, situated on a peninsula surrounded by several scenic inlets and tall hills, all interspersed with a lot of green parkland. The scenery gets more beautiful as you venture farther afield.

We took a drive up the coastal road to the town of Whistler, the site of the 2010 Winter Olympics. The drive itself was worth the trip, with many scenic stops along the way, including waterfalls, spectacular mountain vistas, and dense rain forest.

Whistler is a pleasant, touristy town; unfortunately for us, the summer season was over and the winter ski season hadn't yet started, so there wasn't much to do except gaze in awe at the mountains and heart-stopping scenery, in hopes of spotting Bigfoot, who apparently frequents these areas. There was no sign of him.

Back to Vancouver. Vancouver's craft beer style is similar to Seattle's (which I would describe as Pacific Northwest), though it has many fewer breweries. Nonetheless, there are a number of very good beer bars in all areas of the city. We found the Alibi Room, an extraordinarily friendly, hipster-type watering hole built on the gentrifying edge of the old skid-row area.

They had a good beer list featuring regional beers. I had a chance to sample many of the area beers because there were very few pumpkin beers on the draft list, even though it was September. Thankfully, such spicy concoctions are not as popular in Vancouver as they are in their neighboring city to the south, so the taps were free to feature the local craft beers.

It was at the Alibi Room that we discovered Storm Brewing's *Imperial Flanders Red Ale*. As the brewery notes state, this is a "Belgian-style sour. This crimson hued monster is aged at least a year in the same oak barrels that produced James' insane 12-year-aged lambic. And like the lambic, this beer is not for the faint of heart. Notes of oak, barnyard, and goat complement its high ABV and puckering yet malty sourness. 11% ABV."

All I could say was "Wow." This is the *Duchesse de Bourgogne* on steroids. I was tempted to order another, though at 11%, I knew I couldn't drink that much alcohol. But at last, I had found my exceptional beer of the Pacific Northwest. That was one down.

And then it was time to drive back to Seattle. Once we got past the hour-long wait at the border, the ride back was delightful. The sun was bright, the sky was partly cloudy, and it wasn't raining. We drove the famous Chuckanut Drive, one of the great scenic byways in the country. This highway hugs mountains that spill down to the sea, wandering through the rainforests and small towns with oyster farms. Along the coast, we stopped for

CHAPTER 5: REGIONAL BEERS FROM OTHER AREAS

a seafood lunch, followed by a side trip to San Juan Island and back by ferry. We kept our eyes peeled, but still no yeti.

Finally, on the ferryboat, the ever-present Seattle clouds lifted for a few hours, and that was when we finally got our glimpse of Mt. Rainier in all her glory! The clouds returned by the time we got back to Seattle. We departed the following day. Still no Yeti, but two out of three ain't bad, is it?

CHAPTER 6

BEER PAIRINGS

We pair good wine with good food—so why not beer? For that matter, why not pair good beer with all the things we love, from food, to music, to happy events like weddings and birthdays?

Beer is bubbly, like champagne, and it just cries out to be shared with friends and good times. Here are some of my own experiences in selecting beers to go along with special food, special occasions, music—and even the Oscars!

BEER TASTING—WITH A PURPOSE

YourBeerNetwork.com (August 31, 2011)

We are going to have a huge party in mid-August to celebrate a Very Important Birthday for my husband, Rick. We expect to entertain about 65 people on our deck, overlooking Lake Michigan. Many of our guests will be spending the afternoon at the beach, coming up to the deck to refresh their beers or looking for dinner. Needless to say, I'm in charge of bringing the beer. And as the Beer Doctor, I'd better get it right. My reputation is on the line.

So what beer, and how much?

First, the guest list. Among the 65 guests, 25 are either children or wine drinkers (same thing). At 3.5 beers per person x 40 people, we'll need about 160 servings. Bottles are not allowed on the beach. Cans would do, but our canned beer selection in

CHAPTER 6: BEER PAIRINGS

Indiana is limited to tasteless, mass-market beers. Mini-kegs (5 L) are a possibility, but the selection is limited, and they're hard to keep cold outside. So how about a full keg?

A standard keg, also called a half barrel, contains 15.5 gallons of beer. There are 128 ounces in a gallon, so one keg contains 165 12-ounce servings. OK, one keg will do it.

Next, what beer? Well, it has to be a good beer, something that goes well with burgers and that I would drink myself. A beer that my guests will enjoy. Although I prefer hoppy IPAs, many people don't care for hops. Furthermore, the alcohol content of an IPA is too high for drinking on a hot, summer, three-beer day. Let's keep it to 5% ABV or below.

I don't care for wheat beers, and I am averse to "summer ales," which are often wheat beers flavored with fruit, citrus, or spices. A lighter ale or a lager would be best. The average Midwesterner is used to drinking an insipid, diluted lager (*Bud, Miller Lite, Coors*, etc.), but I don't enjoy them. There are many fine imported lagers, especially of the German variety, but I'm not certain about the availability or expense of an imported keg. I elect to limit my choice to American beers (including Canadian imports). I want a regional microbrew—either a lager or a pale ale—with low alcohol (preferably 5% ABV or less) that's available in a keg. And no Goose Island.

The criteria set, here it was International Hop Day (August 4), and I was tasting lagers and pale ales. To begin with, I selected eight bottled beers from my local beer stores. (I knew my taste buds would tire after eight.) The beers included lagers, pilsners, and pale ales. Rick and I shared the beers and rated them, accompanied by a meal of grilled burgers, first-of-season local corn, salad with local tomatoes, and watermelon.

Here's how they ranked:

First, the lagers were Harp *Irish Lager* (Canada, 4.7%), Bell's *Lager of the Lakes* (Michigan, 5.0%) and Victory *Prima Pils* (Pennsylvania, 5.3%). I had great expectations for Victory *Prima Pils*, a highly regarded pilsner-style beer that has received many awards. It's made with whole hop flowers, using primarily

TO YOUR HEALTH!

German hops. It was "interesting"—not at all a typical pilsner. The fresh hop flavor killed the malty pils taste, and I didn't think my guests would appreciate it. Nor did I. *Harp* and Bell's *Lager of the Lakes* were remarkably well-matched and well-balanced. *Harp* is a classic, but Bell's is more so—with pinpoint carbonation, clear yellow color, and great flavor. It's my pick of this lot.

Next, the pale ales were *Schlafly Pale Ale* (St. Louis, 4.4%), Upland Brewing Co.'s *Helios Pale Ale* (Indiana, 4.8%.), Bell's *Pale Ale* (Michigan, 5.2%), and *Back Road Ale* (Indiana, 5%). The *Schlafly* was insipid and weak, while *Upland* was flavorful with mild hops. Bell's *Pale Ale* did not do well; it was cloudy and bitter. The surprising find was *Back Road Ale*. It's not a pale ale, but it's close to an English bitter. It's a mild, copper-colored ale that's flavored with Fuggles and Styrian Goldings, the same hops used in English bitters. It's easy to drink and has great flavor, but it's not overwhelming. It was our pick of the ales.

Lastly, we tasted the Bell's *Amber Ale* (Michigan, 5.8%) to put it all in perspective. It's sweet, copper colored, and malty, but full of American hops. It's a very good, classic American brown ale. It pairs well with food, but it's too heavy and too hoppy, and it had too much alcohol for our beach party.

Our winning beer was *Back Road Ale*, and our runner-up was Bell's *Lager of the Lakes*. As of this writing, I'm not sure I can get the *Back Road Ale* in a keg, since the brewery favors 1/6-barrel kegs (5.17 gallon pubkegs). I'll know in a week. In the meantime, I'll have to get the burgers, buns, and a *big* cake. I'm afraid I'll also have to feature a case of *PBR* and *MGD 64* to satisfy the young hipsters and the old codgers, respectively.

Happy birthday, Rick!

[Author update: I'm pleased to report that Back Road Brewery provided us with a keg of *Back Road Ale*. It was a hit. Our 70 guests finished almost all of it, along with 40 pounds of burgers, 5 pounds of veggie burgers, and a huge cake. Not one PBR or MGD was drunk, I'm happy to say.]

CHAPTER 6: BEER PAIRINGS

BEER AND BACON CRAWL

by Paul Ciminero with Carol Westbrook
YourBeerNetwork.com (April 8, 2011 and May 9, 2011)

The object: To visit a few Chicago pubs where the food specialty is cured pork products, and to taste the food and accompanying beers.

The results: Our correspondents reviewed 17 beers and accompanying food in two pubs, one gastropub and one brewpub. The reports on two of those locations are listed here.

PART 1: OLD TOWN SOCIAL

Throw objectivity out the window when pub-crawling. Bring a defibrillator to this pork-inspired overdose of food and beer. (Or, at the very least, bring a bottle of Tums.)

    Our first stop on this beer-and-bacon/pork-inspired mini-tour was Old Town Social, a gastropub and charcuterie bar. Located on the corner of North and Cleveland avenues, adjacent to Chicago's Old Town neighborhood, this modern, high-ceilinged establishment has warm, polished heavy wood throughout and is Chicago's latest temple of pig worship. We'd heard the rumblings like the local hype on WGN's *Chicago's Best* program and the numerous write-ups in the local press—so it was time to drink the Kool-Aid (err . . . draft beer) and EAT SOME PIGGY!

Paul: But what is a charcuterie bar? It's an unusual and unique concept, indeed. You've seen sushi bars and oyster bars—but a charcuterie bar? As you attempt to push open the enormous and almost airtight 12' x 4' outer wooden door, you notice a chef standing parallel to the giant window in the inner lobby to your right, slicing and assembling an array of meats and cheeses in a small, sushi bar–like workstation. Welcome! Now, Carol, let's head on in . . . just . . . push . . . the . . . second glass door . . . it's like a freakin' . . . airlock . . . taking both of us a few seconds to budge it . . . then . . . swoosh . . . it opens! Mmmmmmmm . . . the smell of bacon, sausages, curing meats—God, we're starving! Just getting past those two huge doors has stimulated our appetites. OK, Carol, your thoughts . . . .

Carol: You have given me a very easy task, Paul! Pairing beer with some foods can be difficult, but pairing it with pork is a slam dunk. Peasant food requires a peasant drink. Any beer goes with any pork, especially if the pork is cured. And that's probably why pork and beer pairings are so popular in Chicago.

This is my first trip to Old Town Social, and I absolutely love this place! It's a beer bar, it's a whiskey bar, it's a gastropub, it's a neighborhood hangout, and it's also a sports bar. It has great ambiance, and I could sit here for hours and strike up a conversation with just about any denizen.

As a beer bar, it has about a dozen taps with a selection of regional, national, and imported drafts—and the bartender is more than willing to let you sample anything you like. As a gastropub, it's noted for its Sunday brunch, which includes generous servings of pork products.

Paul: So what makes Old Town Social a "gastropub" instead of a pub or a tavern?

Carol: Here's how I would define the drinking scene in Chicago:

Tavern (corner bar, or saloon)—The standard Chicago bar (which serves beer in bottles) or tap (which has beer on draft). It is a neighborhood establishment, limited by its storefront lot size (25-foot lots are the standard in Chicago—hence, "corner bar"), with mass-produced lagers. It may or may not serve snacks or food. Most of the customers are regulars, and it's a place to gather and socialize.

Beer Bar—An establishment with many taps (at least a dozen) and an ever-changing selection of craft and imported beers, a large selection of bottled beer, and few or minimal mass-

CHAPTER 6: BEER PAIRINGS

Paul Ciminero tasting the Bacon Bomb at Paddy Long's Bar during the 2011 Chicago Beer and Bacon pub crawl.

produced beers (*MGD*, *Bud*, etc.). Food is optional. A good example would be the Map Room.

Pub—A gathering place for folks to enjoy good beer and food. (It's kind of like YourBeerNetwork.com.) The draft selection is partially fixed (for the regulars) and partially rotating, with "guest" drafts of craft or imported beers. The food is usually good bar food. Examples would be Duke of Perth (Scottish) or Laschet's Inn (German).

Gastropub—It's all about the food. There *must* be a chef on the premises. As with a restaurant, you usually have to make reservations, so there is a limited number of regulars. The beer menu includes a changing draft list, usually selected to *match* the food. Examples would be Old Town Social, the Publican, and the Gage.

Brewpub—Features the output of a single brewery (with very limited guest beers in bottles or on draft) and almost always includes food. The food should be unique and inspired. Examples of this would be Goose Island and Revolution Brewing.

TO YOUR HEALTH!

Sports Bar—Can be any of the above, but is primarily about providing a *venue to watch the GAME*. The emphasis is on **the Game** or the event itself. Sports bars have satellite feeds of games you can't always get on your TV, and a game is always on (though the sound may be turned off). There is an emphasis on a particular team (or university loyalty) and usually a particular sport. For example, if you stroll down Clark Street, you'll find bars exclusively devoted to watching Cubs baseball games, but you'll also find a bar that features Iowa State, Northwestern, or Notre Dame football, or even a bar or two that primarily feature rugby or European soccer. Some pubs become sports bars when THE game is on! (Like Durkins and Notre Dame football—got it?)

So Old Town Social probably qualifies as a gastropub, while Paddy Long's is a pub, and Revolution Brewing is a brewpub.

Paul: Thanks for clarifying those differences, Carol.

We find a seat at the bar, belly up, and begin questioning the bartender. He's a very affable person, and we have a general idea about where to begin, but even those decisions are extremely hard.

Chef Jared Van Camp sources all his ingredients locally and is a true *Wurstmeister*, grinding, smoking, curing, and aging his meats in-house. You can even order an entire salami (or two) online (selection varies, with three or four being available at any given time), but you have to come in and pick it up when ready, as Old Town doesn't ship any items and some are made-to-order.

The menu consists of a Starter selection, a Sandwich selection (referred to as "Between Bread"), a Sides selection (with everything from a Stilton, Gruyere, and Cheddar Mac 'n' Cheese to Deep-Fried Bread-and-Butter Pickles), a creative Salad selection, and a separate "build-your-own page" (e.g., the Ploughman's Platter).

The Starter selection of either the Grilled Smoked Sausage N Waffles plate, the Three Mini-House Made Hot Dog Plate, the Spicy Duck Wings, and the Crispy Merguez Lamb Sausage

CHAPTER 6: BEER PAIRINGS

Flatbread (with goat cheese, of course) all sound amazing. However, we're here for PIG today.

I didn't notice BACON listed anywhere as a "side," but no worries—it's "Industry Sunday," and that means free bacon with every order of beer, bourbon, or cocktails. YUM!

The Between Bread selection is where we look next, after the bacon no-brainer. I ask, and the barkeep concurs, that we MUST have the Pork Belly Reuben sandwich. Last year I trekked through Chicagoland in search of Chicago's greatest burgers, and I'm sure Jared's Burgers (ground daily from grass-fed beef) are amazing, but I'll return to confirm that soon.

We take the bacon with the Pork Belly Reuben Sandwich and the Charcuterie selection from the Ploughman's Platter page. It seems we're in trouble already, as the Smoked, Salted, and Cured Meats section has 16 items (choose one at $4 or five for $16). I definitely want the Lardo (whipped Italian Butter), the Soppresatta, and the Mortadella.

Now we haggle for 10 minutes over the last two, settling on the Toscano Salame and finally the Chorizo. (The Breseola, an air-dried beef we wanted, was out—and besides, this is a pork outing.) So here's what we finally ordered:

PRIMO:
Pork Belly Reuben Sandwich—The Homer Simpson drool begins flowing down my chin. Now it's all over my shirt, my pants, and the floor. Drool puddles! Gee, maybe I should HAVE A BITE! It's made with succulently moist, 1/3-inch-cut pork belly pastrami, sauerkraut, Russian dressing, Swiss cheese, and soft marble rye. I give Carol a 1-inch square, circle my arms around the plate (like I used to do to keep my siblings from TOUCHING my food as a kid), and begin to devour what is MINE. I think I may have just found the SANDWICH OF THE YEAR. (Yet it's only January 2011.)

Bacon—It's dry and chewy, with loads of flavor. I've discovered Old Town Social's biggest secret: BACON JERKY. OMG, it's really good.

TO YOUR HEALTH!

SECONDO:
The Charcuterie selection arrives on two wooden planks, accompanied by mustard piccalilli relish and grilled bread. Starting on the left plank at the top, here's what we ordered:

1. *Lardo*—I'm sure this stuff is served in heaven on the side with grilled foie gras. (In Hell they serve cold Big Macs on stale, dry bread and cold french fries. It's HELL for Crissakes—what else do you think they'd serve you for eternity?). The Lardo is light as air and fluffy, an explosion of subtle pork flavor that just melts on the tongue. Hmmm... Lardo milkshakes... oh wait, I think Graham Elliot has those at his new carryout joint. To quote Carol here (loudly), "Oh my God, I've died and gone to heaven and am sitting on a white, fluffy cloud."

2. *Toscano Salame*—Ground pork, chunks of fat, red wine, garlic, and pepper. This three-inch-diameter salami has subtle spice notes, with the garlic and chunks of fat adding a slight creaminess to the finish. I take a gulp of the Illinois-made Two Brothers Brewing *Domaine DuPage French Country Ale* and grin like a Cheshire cat.

3. *Chorizo*. When I think "chorizo," I think ground-up Mexican sausage, but here it's an inch-and-a-half-diameter pepperoni-like tube, with loads of flavor and a very spicy finish (courtesy of a healthy dose of dried chilies and smoked paprika).

4. *Mustard Piccalilli Relish and Grilled Bread*—What? No individual mustard(s)? No cornichons? Our bartender tells us that they prefer to serve the wonderfully tart and crunchy mustard-based relish on its own, to cut back the fattiness of the meats. All I can say is, "COME ON, MAN!" They happily supply us with more buttered and grilled bread, but NO MUSTARD! Please, Old Town Social. Mustard! And not the yellow crap found at every hot dog stand under every "L" in Chicago. Gourmet mustards, please! It's really our only criticism of the entire visit.

CHAPTER 6: BEER PAIRINGS

5. *Mortadella*—Originating in the Italian city of Bologna, *Mortadella* has roots that may go back as far as Roman times. It's traditionally a blend of pork with black pepper, myrtle berries, and up to 15 percent neck fat, with pistachios and green olives embedded in it. (The most popular American version is a baloney named Oscar.) Old Town Social's version is four inches in diameter, mild, and flavorful—with pistachios, chunks of lardon (fat), and coriander spice. It's very subtle and tasty.

6. Soppressata—Since this is made with Calabrian (part of my southern Italian roots) chili peppers, garlic, and white wine, I had to try it. Originally, it was made from what's leftover after the pig is slaughtered. Everything was ground up coarsely, encased, hung, and dried for several months. Soppressata is truly Italian "peasant" salami. Here it is dried for a minimum of 60 days and "pressed" into an irregular shape. Jared Van Camp's version is delightful and uses "high quality pork and spices." Reddish in color, with fatty marbling throughout, his Soppressata has well-balanced tanginess with not-too-spicy overtones.

Carol: Are you finally finished? Really? (Just kidding.) Now let me focus on the beer selection. Like most of the patrons, we are here to indulge in the Sunday brunch, which is slanted toward cured meats. We are sharing a plate of charcuterie and the Pork Belly Reuben Sandwich—if you call a one-inch square "sharing"! The guy two seats over is eating sausage and waffles with what looks to be an IPA.

Since it's still early in the day—technically still breakfast time—I'm leaning toward easy-to-drink beverages that are lower in alcohol and maltier in flavor, but without overpowering hops. In addition to low hops, I apply what I think will match well with the food. No insipid "light" beers here. (Well, to be honest, Paul asked to sample the *Victoria* Mexican lager, and the bartender brought us a two-ounce taste—beer rookie!) As always, we're drinking only the drafts. Here's what we sampled:

TO YOUR HEALTH!

1. Rogue's *Dead Guy Ale*. This is a traditional German maibock, somewhat lighter in color. Though bock is usually a spring beer, this beer was actually created for autumn, to celebrate the Mexican Day of the Dead (November 1); hence, the name. It's high in malts and only mildly hoppy, with mostly European hops (40 IBU). It exhibits a hearty flavor, which is great with spicy pork.

2. *Victoria*. As with most Mexican lagers, this beer is brewed in the style of a Vienna lager (as is *Budweiser*). It's made by the Modelo group in Mexico City, and it's only recently become available in the United States. At 4% ABV, it resembles similar Mexican beers—having recently returned from a Cancun vacation, I can guarantee it. What's good about this beer is that it's on draft rather than poured from a bottle, so it's fresher and more drinkable. Otherwise, it's not distinguished, but it's easy to quaff down with a Reuben sandwich.

3. *Wells Bombardier*. This one is my pick of the bar. It's rare to find an English ale on draft in the United States that tastes like a typical English bitter. This one does, and it is a perfect session beer at 4.5% ABV. I could sip it all day while munching on spicy food.

4. Two Brothers Brewing *Domaine DuPage French Country Ale*. This beer was fun and reminiscent of a good Belgian beer, without the yeasty taste. At 5.9% ABV, this was the highest-alcohol beer in this set. Not distinguished on its own, this ale is made for drinking with food and is a perfect complement to charcuterie or a meaty sandwich.

5. *Duchesse de Bourgogne*. Who can't love the Duchesse? This red Flemish ale has moderate alcohol (6.2% ABV) but is low in hops. It is extremely flavorful due to its malty characteristics, unique yeast, and long aging process. This beer is not brewed with fruit, but its taste is reminiscent of a cherry soda. This ale pairs wonderfully with sausage and waffles.

CHAPTER 6: BEER PAIRINGS

    6. *Bell's Two Hearted Ale.* This I chose as my contrast beer—a hoppy American IPA. Just to remind me of my mission, I had a sip of my (current) all-time favorite draft ale. This is a moderately high-alcohol (7% ABV), highly hopped IPA, full of American Centennial hops. It was almost overwhelming compared to all of the other ales we drank at Old Town Social. You could pair this with anything—but then again, I'm biased.

Next stop: Paddy Long's Irish Bar and the Legendary Bacon Bomb. Pass the TUMS. It's going to be a great afternoon!

PART 2—PADDY LONG'S

Not far from the DePaul University campus, in a neighborhood filled with typical Chicago Irish pubs frequented by DePaul University alumni, Paddy Long's stands out. It is a revamped neighborhood pub that is riding the wave of Chicago's current Bacon with Beer obsession.

Entering the front door, the first things you notice are the images of soccer and rugby matches that adorn the walls. How appropriate, as this neighborhood bar's claim to fame is the Bacon Bomb, a five-pound rugby football made from bacon and sausage. So begins our second stop on this pig-inspired excursion. Let the scrum begin!

Paddy Long's Beer and Bacon Pub (that's actually what they call themselves on their website) is located at 1028 W. Diversey Parkway in Chicago, a block west of Sheffield Avenue in the New Town neighborhood. They've got a large selection of draft beers and ales (not surprisingly, I count 18 handles—Carol's favorite arbitrary number of taps), an outstanding bottle list, and an array of single malts. Carol gives us some more background.

Carol: This one was my pick, both for the bacon and for the nostalgia. I used to live next door to the establishment when it was an old Chicago tap (Lawry's) with a commercial lager beer selection and occasional food. Lawry's had been in the neighborhood for 73 years, serving mediocre beer and charging $7 for all-you-can-eat deep-fried fish (Friday) or chicken (Saturday). Yes, our wedding party ended up there for fried chicken some 12 years ago.

The new owners, Chris and Pat, took over the bar in 2007 and cleaned it up immediately. The ambiance is great now. It still has a homey, Chicago pub feel, with many regular patrons, friendly people, and a great beer list. They are still serving greasy food, but with a difference—it's GOOD grease, and that's why I dragged Paul here.

Paul: The food is your basic pub fare: burgers and fries, wings, nachos, beer-battered fish-and-chips, classic sandwiches, and even *Guinness* Beef Stew, but with a top-heavy, bacon-inspired theme. There are bacon specialty appetizers (deep-fried bacon and bacon-wrapped dates) and main courses—the half-pound bacon BLT for $12.95 and the notorious Bacon Bomb sandwich for $9.95. We'll get to the actual Bacon Bomb shortly.

Paddy's offers a Beer and Bacon pairing on Wednesdays (7:00–9:00 p.m.) and on weekends (Saturdays and Sundays from 2:00–4:00 p.m.). It features five cuts of bacon with five seasonal beers for $36. Be warned: this is Paddy Long's most popular draw, and you can only book reservations online. They limit the reservations to around 35 people, and currently, they are sold out five weeks in advance.

Carol: We didn't sign up for the Beer and Bacon pairing—at $36 for five mini-drafts and five tastes of bacon, it's a bit pricey. The folks next to us had purchased half-price tickets on Groupon, so they shared their pairing lists and a few sips of their beers. As I said, it's a friendly pub.

Paul: Having just left Old Town Social, I was pretty stuffed, but fortunately, Paddy's makes a Bacon Bomb sandwich and fries for $9.95, so I ordered that. The actual Bacon Bomb is five pounds of ground pork, sausage, nasty bits, and spices, wrapped in sweet smoked bacon. The finished product looks like a peewee football, and it serves five to seven people.

Or you can attempt the gluttonous Bacon Bomb Challenge. (Yes, I'm sure Adam Richman will come with the Travel Channel's

CHAPTER 6: BEER PAIRINGS

Man v. Food show soon; how can he resist?). The challenge is to consume the entire "Bomb" with a large batch of fries in 45 minutes—then it's free, plus you get a T-shirt and are added to the pub's Wall of Fame. This is cheesy commercialism at its finest. The manager told us they serve 15 to 20 Bacon Bombs daily. (Thank goodness there is a hospital three blocks away.)

The sandwich version was an inch-circular cut off the Bomb, open-faced and served on a bun with a side of lettuce, onion, tomatoes, and another of wonderfully crisp, tasty fries. It was very peppery, with loads of spice and flavor, but somewhat dry. I expected it to be oily or at least have more moisture in it. It makes you want to drink a lot of beer with it. Hmmm . . . I'm on to something here.

Carol: On to the beer. Paddy's draft list is unique and not at all what you'd expect from an "Irish" bar in Chicago. There were only two Irish beers on draft, *Kilkenny* and *Guinness*, and only a few hoppy ales. I would characterize the beer list as "dark-and-light." There were quite a number of dark beers—porters, stouts, and smoked beers—as well as a generous number of lager-style beers. Why the mix? Probably because the dark beers go so well with the smoky flavor of bacon, and the lagers . . . well, Chicagoans LOVE their lagers.

We tasted some of the beers recommended on the bacon-pairing list for that week. It is, literally, a black-and-white selection. My descriptions of the brews are listed by number below, with Paul's comments on the food pairing throughout.

1. Mikkeller *Beer Geek Bacon.* This is a smoked malt imperial stout produced by a relatively young (five years old), very small brewery in Denmark noted for unusual beers, especially those that are barrel aged and that contain coffee. An imperial stout has a higher alcohol content due to the fact that it is brewed with more malt than is a usual stout; in this case, the malt is heavily smoked, so you can taste the smoke as well as the coffee. I found it too bitter for my taste, and the high alcohol

TO YOUR HEALTH!

content (7.5% ABV) intensified the bitterness. However, it's definitely unique and worth a taste. The Bacon Bomb is well-paired with this.

Paul: I would have to say that any malted beverage called *Beer Geek Bacon* stout got my attention. It works perfectly to swill with swine.

2. *Stone Smoked Porter*. This is a porter, meaning it's a dark ale, not as dense as a stout. It is lightly hopped, but the peat-smoked taste comes through. It's quite drinkable at 5.8% ABV, and it goes well with bacon/pork sausage, though again, you can get tired of the peat flavor. I tasted a beer similar to this in Islay, Scotland: *Black Rock Ale*, which was made from peat-smoked malt that would otherwise be used to make Scotch whiskey. I personally think that making Scotch whiskey is a better use of the malts, but go ahead—it's a good lunchtime drink with strong-flavored, grilled, or smoked food.

Paul: It was paired with the Brown Sugar Bacon, and it perfectly complemented the sweetness of that bacon.

3. Metropolitan *Krankshaft*. This was your pick, Paul, because (a) you love lagers and (b) the brewery is near your house. Fair enough. Close brewery = extremely fresh beer, and I second that. It is a German-style beer, similar to those brewed in Cologne, though some wheat was thrown in. It has a low bitterness from its Santiam hops (28 IBU), and the alcohol is only 5% ABV, so it's easy to drink lots of this beer, even out of the bottle (heaven forbid)! It's a great alternative if you're used to drinking *Bud*, *Corona*, *MGD*, etc. and want something much tastier.

Paul: Actually, Carol, I prefer IPAs to lagers, in general, but I'm just a "beer novice" and wanted to try the local neighborhood guys' wares. On the tasting menu that day, it was matched up with Irish Bacon.

CHAPTER 6: BEER PAIRINGS

    4. *Trumer Pils.* This is brewed by an Austrian-run California brewery. Nice and somewhat light at 4.8% ABV, I don't think it's a perfect pairing for bacon, but on the other hand, it's a good beer for lunch. The couple sitting next to us poured me a little of this, and I sampled the Peppercorn Applewood Bacon paired with it.

Paul: The Peppercorn Applewood Bacon was very smoky and spicy. Paddy's pairing-tasting notes said the Austrian-style pilsner was a "classic thirst-quenching pils that put out the fire" of the bacon. I agree with Carol that it was, in fact, a mismatch. This pilsner would work with sweet bacon, but not with this one. Spice and citrus work well together, so the *Alpha King* with citrusy American hops would have been my choice.

Carol: Two other beers of note that we did not taste that day (and one I tasted and really loved) are listed below:

    5. *Hirter Morchl.* This is a dunkel lager that's described as having "smooth, roasty flavor with a crisp lager finish" and 5% ABV. I admit that I tasted this a few days later and found it was very nice, smooth, and easy to drink. This is classic Austrian lager.

    6. Unita Crooked Line *Labyrinth Black Ale.* This is a huge Imperial stout from a Utah microbrewery. It is aged for six months in oak barrels, rendering 13.2% ABV.

    7. *Duvel Green.* Finally, my "contrast beer"—*Duvel Green*—turned out to be the most noteworthy beer I drank that day at Paddy's. I absolutely loved this new Belgian beer! Its parent beer, *Duvel,* is a lovely Belgian light ale that was only available in bottles, since its unique flavor derives from the fact that it is bottle conditioned (or aged). This beer comes off fermentation and is immediately kegged and delivered, so it's young and "green." It's a bit cloudy and tastes similar to a really good home brew. The superb *Duvel* yeast taste and hops are apparent, and it's very drinkable. It's a stretch to say it goes well with smoky bacon (it doesn't).

In summary, head over to Paddy Long's if you want to taste some unique, dark, and smoky beers that you're unlikely to find anywhere else in town, and if you have a hankering to pair them with pork products.

Paul: My head is pounding, my stomach is stuffed, and we still have two hours before we join Carol's husband for dinner at Owen & Engine pub. I've got a great idea: I'll drag Carol over to Revolution Brewing for some Bacon Fat Popcorn and four of their IPAs in a taster. We are just taking one or two small sips at this point, and stamina has its limits, especially with my middle-aged carcass today. Even with at least two quarts of water to counter the small amount of alcohol I've actually ingested, I'm fatigued. But a good soldier marches on, even though his "march" may have slowed to a crawl. Today's excursion has become a crawl, in every sense of the word.

MOONLIGHT, MUSIC, AND A GLASS OF … BEER

YourBeerNetwork.com (November 6, 2012)

It's opera season! For some, fall means football, a new TV season, Halloween, or pumpkin ales. But it's also the start of the opera season. I am a big fan of opera. I enjoy the performances, with their extravagant sets and costumes; I love the melodrama, which brings tears to my eyes, and I love the bigger-than-life opera superstars. But mostly, I love the music—the most profound and passionate ever produced on the planet.

I am not alone. There are many opera lovers out there, including a disproportionate number of doctors. Why do doctors like opera so much? Is it the pathos of the story? The humanity of the characters? Or is it the snob appeal of the opera experience, with its exorbitant ticket prices limiting attendance to those who can afford to drink champagne at intermission?

CHAPTER 6: BEER PAIRINGS

At one time, I considered writing a book that paired the great opera arias with the wines of the world. Sadly, I don't know much about wine—but I DO know about beer! So I've put together beer selections to accompany famous opera arias. Someday, when opera reaches an even higher level of snobbery, intermission will feature good beers, as well as champagne. Till then you can watch the arias on YouTube—and you'll have to get your own beer. So sit back, tune in to YouTube, grab a brewski, and enjoy.

At the end of each section, I give my favorite video of the selected aria and provide the YouTube link. You can type in the link or search YouTube using the name of the aria and the artist.

1. **The best of both worlds: *La Bohème* and a Belgian Trappist ale**

    We'll start with one of the most beloved scenes in all of opera, Act I of *La Bohème*. Here, Rodolfo comes across Mimi for the first time, illuminated by the light of the moon—and it is love at first sight. He takes her hand, professes his love, and asks her name (in his aria "*Che gelida manina,*" meaning "Your cold hand."). She replies, "They call me Mimi" (in her aria "*Si, mi chiamano Mimi*"). The sweetness of the encounter is all the more intense because you know that in the end, she is going to die before they really get together.

    The story of *La Bohème* resonates through the ages. Les bohèmes—the bohemians—are a group of twenty-somethings who are trying to make a go of it in Paris, living in an unheated garret and falling in and out of love. Rodolfo and Mimi! Their morals may be loose, but their love is pure. In the end, they are separated by her tragic death due to consumption—a disease brought on by poverty. (In the musical *Rent*, a modern incarnation of this story, it is AIDS that does *him* in.) In the YouTube link, the aria is sung by the best tenor of the 20th century, the late Luciano Pavarotti. You will understand why he was called the master of the high C.

TO YOUR HEALTH!

To accompany these paired arias, we will look for a beer that stands out. It has to be sensual and intense, with its own morality. Of course it has to be brewed by Trappist monks. We want a brew that is strong and flavorful but bittersweet, with almost unattainable promise. My preferences would be *Trappistes Rochefort 10*, a Belgian abbey beer—some say the best beer in the world. For this, it is a tie with *Chimay Blue*, which is also a good pick for this opera.

So enjoy the world's best opera—sung by the world's greatest tenor—while drinking the world's best beer. I cry every time I hear this music. If this doesn't make you an opera lover—and a beer lover—then you are hopeless (hopless?).

THE ARIA: "Che gelida manina," from a 1986 performance of *La Bohème* (Giacomo Puccini), sung by Pavarotti and d'Amico. This recording of the Italian opera has the benefit of English subtitles!

http://www.youtube.com/watch?v=OkHGUaB1Bs8

2. ***The Magic Flute* and a German lager**

Mozart was a master of melody, and his operas reflect that fact. As with a good musical, you could almost sing along. Though many German operas are heavy and tragic (e.g., Wagner's Ring Cycle), Mozart's operas tend to be light and playful, with happy endings. *The Magic Flute* is my favorite. It is a fantasy, involving magic and fairies and spells and talking animals.

One of the subplots involves the talking bird, Papageno, who is searching throughout the show for his soul mate, his other half, without whom he will die. Finally, he finds her, and the story can end happily. Their meeting is depicted in the playful duet, "Papageno Papagena." The music will delight you. You'll find you want to sing along to the "Pop Pop Poppa" of the lyrics and raise a stein or two with your friends.

CHAPTER 6: BEER PAIRINGS

What's best to drink? Why, a German lager! Try a *Warsteiner* or *Spaten Pils*; or better yet, an Oktoberfest beer such as *Spaten Oktoberfest*. Don't care for lagers? Try a good English bitter (*Wells Bombardier* is my current favorite). Yes, any good session beer will do, even a *Guinness*—but don't stop at one.

THE ARIA: "Papageno Papagena," from *The Magic Flute*, by Wolfgang Amadeus Mozart.

http://www.youtube.com/watch?v=J7SggJWtB2A&feature=related

3. **"The Queen of the Night" (from *The Magic Flute*), paired with the Queen of American Ales**

   The other side of the *Magic Flute* involves a villain, the Queen of the Night, who is just pure evil. Of course, goodness triumphs over evil in the end, but not without a spectacular aria sung by the Queen. This is one of the most difficult arias that a diva can sing, requiring agility of voice and extraordinarily high range, extending to high F! This will knock your socks off. Go, Mozart!

   The Queen is an intimidating bully—complex and compelling, deep and bitter, but not without charm. We need a drink that hits the high notes: passionate, scary, complex, and demanding full attention. Sound familiar? I'll go with a very hoppy American IPA: *Harpoon IPA*, *Bell's Two Hearted Ale*, Victory's *HopDevil IPA*, or anything from Dogfish Head or Stone. Arguably, U.S. brewing is at its best with IPAs, the Queen of American beers.

   THE ARIA: Diana Damrau sings the "Queen of the Night" aria from the Magic Flute (Wolfgang Amadeus Mozart) at the Royal Opera House in London.

   http://www.youtube.com/watch?v=C2ODfuMMyss

4. ***Boris Godunov*: a dark opera needs a dark beer.**

Italian operas are about moonlight, love, intrigue, and thwarted love; and German operas are about magic and sorcery; but Russian operas are about politics. Intrigue and psychological torment factor heavily, as they do in Russian novels. *Boris Godunov* is Mussorgsky's masterpiece, and I won't even try to explain the lengthy and complicated plot.

Suffice it to say that it is about the life of Tsar Boris Godunov during his reign from 1598 to 1606 and his struggles to defend the empire from internal and external threats. Boris usurped the throne by assassinating his brother-in-law, Dmitry—the true heir of Tsar Ivan the Terrible—and he is wracked with remorse. As the political intrigues heighten throughout the story, so does his conscience continue to haunt him, gradually driving him to hallucinations, insanity, and eventually, death. There is a wonderful scene (the clock scene) in which the chimes of a ticking clock remind him of his mortality; the clock is echoed in his death scene, when he imagines his funeral bells.

Here we will view the death scene, when Boris hands his throne over to his son, agonizes over his unforgiven sin, and breathes his last. In general, opera showcases the tenor and soprano voices, and there are few outstanding arias for bass singers (basso profundo). This is one of them, and it is sung by one of the world's outstanding bass voices, Nicolai Ghiaurov.

This aria calls for a strong, dark, heavy, and bitter beer—a beer to cry in. A barley wine, perhaps. A Baltic-style beer. My two recommendations are these:

1) *Old Rasputin Russian Imperial Stout* (North Coast Brewing), 75 IBUs, 9% ABV.

2) *Sinebrychoff Porter.* A Baltic porter from Finland, hard to find but worth the effort. 7.2% ABV.

CHAPTER 6: BEER PAIRINGS

THE ARIA: Nicolai Ghiaurov sings "Boris' Death Scene" from Boris Godunov (Modest Mussorgsky).

http://www.youtube.com/watch?v=B4vxQiA8Ghk&feature=related

5. *Carmen* **and the** *Duchesse*

Carmen, by Georges Bizet, is one of the best-known operas because of its memorable music. Who doesn't know "The Toreador Song"? Although the opera is sung in French, it takes place in Spain. It is a story of seduction, love, outlaws, and murder. Carmen, the heroine, is a beautiful but lawless Roma woman. She uses her powers of seduction to get her way and bypass the law, but she is herself seduced.

Carmen sings and dances the spirited "Habanera" in a tavern. The lyrics proclaim, "Love knows no laws." She catches the eye of a soldier, Don José, whom she seduces. When she is thrown in prison, she uses him to help her escape, thereby making him an outlaw as well. He deserts and joins her gang of smugglers. In the meantime, she is swept off her feet by the Toreador. José has lost everything, and he kills Carmen in a jealous rage. Everyone loses in this tragedy.

We must pair this delightful aria with a beer that resembles Carmen herself: a beautiful and passionate woman, sweet but seductive, assertive and compelling. Yes, it's the *Duchesse de Bourgogne*, a Belgian Flemish-style ale. It's a surprising drink because it tastes of cherries and raspberries, though it is not made with fruit. It's seductive—try drinking just one.

We have paired a Flemish ale, brewed in Belgium, with a French opera about a Roma woman in Spain. As we end this column we show, once again, that beer, like opera, is truly international!

THE ARIA: In this 1984 movie production of Georges

Bizet's Carmen, Julia Migenes-Johnson sings a very sexy and flirtatious "Habanera."

http://www.youtube.com/watch?v=_8y1dj7bvjE

This column is dedicated to my friend and inspiration, Fred Tasker, master wine columnist for *The Miami Herald* and WLRN radio; and his beautiful daughter, Annie, my daughter-in-law, a journalist and mezzo-soprano.

WINE FOR THE WEDDING FEAST— AND BEER, TOO

YourBeerNetwork.com (February 24, 2014)

When I'm asked to bring beer to an event or to host a party, it goes without saying that the beer is expected to be good. And when that event is a wedding, the beer selection has to be perfect!

In July of 2013, I hosted the rehearsal dinner for my son's wedding. We were expecting 76 guests for this meal at Tim Schafer's Cuisine in Morristown, New Jersey. Because the restaurant is a BYOB establishment, I had to purchase the beer and wine to complement a delicious but eclectic menu. The beer would be easy, but I don't know much about wine—and since the bride's father was a nationally known wine expert, my reputation was on the line.

For 76 guests, I estimated 2 bottles of beer (about 6½ cases) and half of a bottle of wine per person, or about 38 bottles (meaning at least 3 cases). The entrée selections (listed below) included fish, shellfish, beef, and vegetarian, with flavors ranging from mild to spicy. This was a menu that I could not complement with just two beer choices (lager and ale) and two wine choices (red and white). The drink selections would have to be just as varied. This was going to be a challenge!

Here are the menus I was working with:

CHAPTER 6: BEER PAIRINGS

Gene and Annie

MAIN COURSE SELECTIONS FOR REHEARSAL DINNER

Tim Schafer's Cuisine, Morristown, New Jersey

St. Peter's Fish Fillet
Maryland lump crab meat, vine-ripened red tomatoes, capers, and scallions sauté finished with a citrus beer-blanc and creamy spinach scented risotto

TO YOUR HEALTH!

Medallions of Filet Mignon
Grilled filet mignon served over Gorgonzola cheese, enhanced by a cabernet sauvignon reduction and seasonal vegetable medley

Wild Mushroom Ravioli
Fresh pasta filled with a blend of wild mushrooms and cheeses, with a light Parmesan herb cream sauce

Kettle Cooked Short Ribs of Beef
Enticed by a *Guinness* stout, BBQ sauce, plated with roasted corn, whipped potatoes, and sautéed vegetables

Creole-Style Jambalaya
Tim's rendition of this classic New Orleans-style stew with chicken, andouille, and garlic herb sausages, Tasso ham, and vegetables, blended with our special Cajun spices and topped with rice pilaf

The beer selection was straightforward, especially since I had help from the bride and groom, who joined me to taste beer at the Electric City Craft Brew Fest, described in YBN, May 15, 2013. You may recall our specifications: we would select only regional brands available in bottles or cans, with a relatively low alcohol content of 5% ABV or less. We would include both lagers and ales, and all had to be delicious and pair well with food.

When it came time to purchase the beer, we came pretty close to our original selections, though some were unavailable. I could not locate a case of Old Forge's *T-Rail Pale Ale*, and Victory's *Saison* was no longer in season, so it was replaced by Victory's *Summer Love Ale*. A better choice for a wedding, don't you think?

I had to relax my low-alcohol specification, since most IPAs have a higher % ABV due to their higher malt content. Because the bride's family was from Michigan, I included two cases of *Bell's Two Hearted Ale*, which is brewed in Michigan and is one of my favorites. I purchased seven cases of beer overall.

Here's the beer list, which was distributed along with the menu to all the guests:

CHAPTER 6: BEER PAIRINGS

GENE & ANNIE REHEARSAL DINNER
JULY 5, 2013
FEATURED BEER

Summer Love, Victory Brewing Company, Downingtown, Pennsylvania

A light-bodied ale, with the sublime, earthy familiarity of noble European hops, backed up by fresh, clean, German malts, *Summer Love Ale* ends with a surprising burst of lemony refreshment from fistfuls of American whole flower hops. 5.2% ABV.

Susquehanna Brewing Co. Selections, Pittston, Pennsylvania

Goldencold Lager is a German-inspired beer. Brewed with pilsner malt and a small amount of Sauermalz to bring out a traditional, rounded note, Bavarian Hallertau Tradition and Perle hops make for a crisp, classic, and nuanced bitterness. 5% ABV.

Pils Noir is an innovative black pilsner made from Pearl (winter) barley; malted by Munton's, CaraMalt, and Crystal malts; and prepared using a unique, husk-free milling process. The beer is then naturally darkened using the classic Czech technique of decoction mashing. Hopped with Oregon Willamette, Mt. Hood, and Washington hops, and finished with noble Czech Saaz for a fine aroma. 4.9% ABV.

6th Generation Stock Ale features a unique blend of Pearl, Tipple, Crystal, and Maris Otter malts. It uses only hops from Oregon, mostly grown by Goschie Farms in the Willamette Valley, including Mt. Hood, Sterling, and whole-cone Liberty hops. 44 IBUs, 5.5% ABV.

HopFive IPA contains a blend of five hop varieties: Bravo; Willamette; Mount Hood; English Progress; and as-harvested, whole-cone Liberty hops. It presents a floral, pine-like aroma and full hop flavor. 6% ABV.

TO YOUR HEALTH!

Exit 16, **Flying Fish Brewing Co., wild rice double IPA**

Exit 16 on the New Jersey Turnpike takes you into the Hackensack Meadowlands, which are usually identified with landfills and pipelines but are also an amazingly diverse ecosystem providing vital animal and plant habitats. In a nod to a once common food plant here, the beer is brewed with wild rice, as well as with organic brown and white rice. This double IPA is brewed with five hops, then dry-hopped with Chinook and Citra hops to create a nose that hints at tangerine, mango, papaya, and pine. 62 IBUs, 8% ABV.

Bell's Two Hearted Ale, **Bell's Brewery, Kalamazoo, Michigan**

This IPA is hopped exclusively with the Centennial hop varietal from the Pacific Northwest; massive additions in the kettle and again in the fermenter lend their characteristic grapefruit and pine resin aromas. A significant malt body balances this hop presence; together with the signature fruity aromas of Bell's house yeast, this leads to a remarkably drinkable American-style India Pale Ale. 7% ABV.

Now on to the wines. I knew these were going to be a challenge, since my knowledge of wine is limited and so was my budget. I called on Fred Tasker, the father of the bride, who put together a list of moderately priced wines from tasting notes in some of his recent wine columns. He wrote to me:

> I've tried to suggest safe wines with no quirks or hard edges. Pretty much every white-wine drinker likes chardonnay, since it's very fruity. You'll see that the two Kendall-Jackson chards are purposely made quite differently from each other.
>
> The sauvignon blancs are from New Zealand. They're crisp and lively and very popular, although not everybody likes them. Nice contrast, though.
>
> For the reds, pinot noir is softer than cabernet sauvignon, and a lot of people don't like cabs. I also added some nice Italian reds as a contrast.

CHAPTER 6: BEER PAIRINGS

The list was an excellent mix of wine styles that would mate well with the food we were serving, and all were in a modest price range of under $25 a bottle. Due to the vagaries of Pennsylvania law, however, I had to buy wine in our state stores, so my selection was limited. I had no problem with Fred's chardonnay recommendations, but I came up dry for his other selections.

However, I did rely on his varietal selections—New Zealand sauvignon blanc, California pinot noir, and Tuscan reds. Yes, our state store carried many different choices among these varieties, but I still had no way to tell a good bottle from a bad one, as there were no posted ratings. I couldn't drag Fred out to Pennsylvania, buy a few dozen bottles, and taste them all—though it was tempting. Clearly, I needed a personal wine critic to accompany me.

I solved this problem with the Internet. I purchased an iPad app called Wine Ratings from *Wine Spectator,* the wine-reviewing magazine that has one of the most extensive collections of wine ratings available. To use this app, one enters the name of the wine and the vintage year, and one is given the Wine Spectator rating (if available), from 0 to 100. I took my iPad along to the state store and went through the shelves, getting the ratings for all of the bottles in the selected varietals. I got a few odd looks in the store, but it enabled me to narrow the list to wines rated 90 or higher for under $25. Success! Even Fred liked my picks. I purchased 39 bottles.

Here is the wine list, which was distributed along with the menu to all the guests:

GENE & ANNIE REHEARSAL DINNER
JULY 5, 2013
FEATURED WINE

White Wines

2011 Kendall-Jackson *Vintner's Reserve Chardonnay,* California

This wine has a hint of oak and rich tropical fruit flavors, including ripe pineapples. Creamy and smooth.

TO YOUR HEALTH!

2011 Kendall-Jackson *AVANT* chardonnay, California

This has intense fruit aromas and flavors of Granny Smith apples and lemons. Lean and crisp.

2008 Staete Landt *Estate Grown Marlborough* sauvignon blanc, Marlborough, New Zealand

This wine is vivid, bracing, and brimming with lime-tinged grapefruit and guava flavors that persist into the long, distinctive finish.

Red Wines

2011 Rodney Strong Vineyards *Reserve Pinot,* Russian River Valley, California

This wine has a hint of oak, black plum, and blueberry flavors; and a smooth, long finish.

2009 Tenuta La Badiola *642° Maremma Toscana Reserve*, Tuscany, Italy

Squarely in the Italian camp, this wine adds a sour cherry component to the mix of flavors, including black currant and raspberry. It has good acidity and firm yet well-integrated tannins, with fine length.

2009 *Villa Antinori Toscana*, Tuscany, Italy

Black currant, bilberry, violet, and spice flavors align in this luscious red, which is well-balanced and integrated, with a lingering sweet fruit and spice aftertaste. It is a blend of sangiovese, cabernet sauvignon, merlot, and syrah.

The rehearsal dinner came off smoothly, as planned. The party favors included bottle openers and corkscrews, personalized with the couple's name and the wedding date. Surprisingly, the leftovers included only one case of beer, which the groom, his groomsmen, and some of his friends were happy to dispose of later that night. Nevertheless, the young couple were married the following day and are living happily ever after.

CHAPTER 6: BEER PAIRINGS

OSCAR PAIRINGS

Carol Westbrook, January 19, 2014

The Academy Awards 2014 nominations for Best Picture were announced last week. I am trying to see all of them before the winners are announced at the Oscars ceremony on March 2. So far I've seen almost all of them, accompanied by popcorn and a coke—and they're all so good that I plan to see each of them at least once more. But I'll wait until they're available for home viewing on Netflix or on DVD, when I can kick back and enjoy them with a cold beer—and popcorn, of course.

For those of you who plan to do the same, here are the beers I recommend for each of these wonderful films. In case you haven't seen the films yet, I've provided my synopsis of each film and a link to the trailer. Or you can find the trailer yourself by Googling the name of the film. Enjoy the movies!

AMERICAN HUSTLE
http://www.americanhustle-movie.com/site/#videos

This film is about a con man, Irving Rosenfeld (Christian Bale) who, with his partner, Sydney Prosser (Amy Adams), becomes involved in an FBI scam to entrap politicians and mafiosi. Although the movie is fictional, it is based on the true story of the Abscam scandal, which took down the mayor of Newark and several members of Congress. Directed by David O. Russell, it's a wild ride, with an excellent cast that will have you at the edge of your seat the entire show.

A classic American story of con men and political corruption—what pairs better with that than a classic American IPA? There are so many excellent ones, including drafts from your nearby microbrewery. For bottled beers in this genre, my picks are Harpoon's *Harpoon IPA*, Bell's *Two Hearted Ale*, and Dogfish Head's *60 Minute IPA*.

TO YOUR HEALTH!

CAPTAIN PHILLIPS

http://www.captainphillipsmovie.com/site/#videos

Captain Phillips recounts the true story of the capture by Somali pirates of the merchant ship *Alabama* and its commanding officer, Captain Richard Phillips, who was taken hostage. Although we're all familiar with the story because of its extensive media coverage, seeing it on film is another experience.

Particularly noteworthy about the film is the intense interaction between Phillips and the Somali pirate captain, Muse. The film is directed by Paul Greengrass, and all the action takes place on the open sea, where most of it was filmed as well, lending it a very realistic quality. Tom Hanks gives one of his most memorable performances as Captain Phillips, but he meets his acting match in Barkhad Abdi, a native Somali who plays Muse in his first movie role. Both were nominated for Academy Awards for their performances.

For this true yarn of captains and piracy, I would drink what captains drink: *Boston Lager*, of course, from Samuel Adams Brewery. I would imagine that pirates drink *Guinness* stout, from a mug, of course.

DALLAS BUYERS CLUB

http://www.focusfeatures.com/dallas_buyers_club

Another film this year based on true events, *Dallas Buyers Club* tells the fascinating and surprisingly engaging story of Ron Woodroof, a rodeo hustler in Dallas who was diagnosed with AIDS in 1985. Disappointed and disillusioned by the pharmaceutical industry's unwillingness to freely provide experimental AIDS medications, he started an organization that imported and sold alternative AIDS drugs. Woodroof took on the pharmaceutical industry, the medical establishment, and his own homophobic prejudices to keep the Dallas Buyers Club providing these medications to his newfound friends, the AIDS patients.

CHAPTER 6: BEER PAIRINGS

Matthew McConaughey was nominated for Best Actor for his portrayal of Ron Woodroof. The film was directed by Jean-Marc Vallée.

Of course we will be drinking a classic Texas craft beer when we watch this film. And what says "Texas" more than *Shiner Bock*? A malty, American-style dark lager, flavored with German hops, you can drink this one from the bottle.

GRAVITY

http://gravitymovie.warnerbros.com/#/videos/main-trailer

Gravity is the portrayal of a space-walk accident that leaves Dr. Ryan Stone (Sandra Bullock) alone in space, between two space stations, without communication with Earth and with little chance for rescue. The entire story takes place in zero gravity, and the film is so realistic that you feel you're there, floating in free fall. The immensity of space and the views of Earth are mesmerizing, particularly when viewed in 3-D. Directed by Alfonso Cuarón, the movie also stars George Clooney.

For this movie, we want a low-gravity beer with a sweet finish. That means a low-alcohol wheat beer, flavored with spices and fruit. There are many choices, and most are summer beers. Here are some suggestions: Bell's *Oberon Ale*, a classic wheat beer with an orange finish (contributed by the yeast); and Kona Brewing Co.'s *Wailua Ale*, a wheat beer brewed with passion fruit.

HER

http://www.herthemovie.com/#/home

Like most good futuristic sci-fi stories, *Her* is compelling because the future it portrays is eerily similar to the present. In this future version of Los Angeles, crowds of people walk about, talking or texting on their phones, oblivious to others and alone together. One lonely soul—Theodore Twombly, played by Joaquin Phoenix—finds love and companionship in his computer operating systems. This film is directed by Spike Jonze.

Scarlett Johansson's voice won my heart as Samantha, the intelligent operating system who is all woman. This calls for a girly beer that is sweet and light, like Samantha. Among the multiple options are Dogfish Head's *Festina Peche*, a 4.5% ABV Berliner Weisse flavored with tart peach; and Cigar City Brewing's *Pineapple Kolsch*, which is flavored with (you guessed it) pineapple, and only 5% ABV.

NEBRASKA
http://www.nebraskamovie.com/videos.php

An aging and unhappy old man, Woody Grant, believes he has won a million-dollar sweepstakes. He embarks on a cross-country trip from Montana to Nebraska to claim his winnings, accompanied by his estranged son. Along the way, both learn more about each other and develop a closeness and respect they never shared before. *Nebraska* is directed by Alexander Payne and stars Bruce Dern as Woody and Will Forte as his son.

The beer: *Budweiser, Coors,* or *Miller Lite*—drunk from the bottle, as they do in the film.

PHILOMENA
http://philomenamovie.com/videos.html

Philomena, like many of the other Oscar nominees this year, is a true story. It tells the story of a 70-year-old woman's search for the child she was forced to give away for adoption when she was an unwed mother of 18, living in Ireland. Judi Dench is spectacular as Philomena, but of course, she is usually spectacular in any role she attempts. *Philomena* was directed by Stephen Frears.

This movie is a human-interest story that starts in England and ends in the United States. The perfect beer pairing is *Fat Tire Amber Ale*, a classic American craft beer that was inspired by a trip to Europe. According to the brewers, the beer has "a sense of balance and . . . pairs well with people." As does Judi Dench, the leading lady who has been nominated for Best Actress.

CHAPTER 6: BEER PAIRINGS

12 YEARS A SLAVE
http://www.12yearsaslave.com/

Directed by Steve McQueen, *12 Years a Slave* is a historical drama based on an 1853 memoir of the same name by Solomon Northrup. Northrup, an African American, was born a free man but later kidnapped and sold into slavery. The movie tells the realistic and often disturbing story of his years in slavery and his eventual return to freedom. Northrup is played by Chiwetel Ejiofor, who was nominated for Best Actor for his performance.

For this film, we looked for a beer—preferably one from the South—that was strong but required patience to age. Lexington Brewing and Distilling Company's *Kentucky Bourbon Barrel Ale* hit the spot. This beer is aged for up to six weeks in freshly decanted bourbon barrels and is very strong (8.2% ABV), with a marvelous finish, like the movie.

THE WOLF OF WALL STREET
http://www.thewolfofwallstreet.com/

The Wolf of Wall Street is based on the true story of Jordan Belfort. It chronicles his rise to wealthy stockbroker and his eventual fall due to crime, corruption, and the federal government—as he lives the high life of drugs, women, yachts, bribery, and money, money, money. Leonardo DiCaprio is the Wolf, in one of the best performances of his career. The film is directed by Martin Scorsese.

This movie is harsh, over-the-top, full of foul language, and thoroughly entertaining. We needed a very hoppy double IPA to drink with this film. *Stone Ruination IPA*, at 100+ IBUs and 8.2% ABV, was the obvious pick. An alternative suggestion is Dogfish Head's *90 Minute IPA*, at 9% ABV and 90 IBUs.

Guinness *chocolate cake*

CHAPTER 7

COOKING WITH BEER

I was first introduced to the pleasures of beer as an ingredient during a trip to Brittany, in the North of France, where I first tasted *Moules-frites*. These freshly caught mussels are steamed in white wine or my favorite, Belgian white beer. They're served up with what the French call *pommes frites*, or what we Americans call french fries.

Beer may not be as versatile as wine in cooking, but it can add body and character to a dish. Furthermore, it's a great leavening agent for baking, and some beer styles—stouts in particular—work well in desserts.

With the growth of craft beer, there is increased interest in cooking with beer, and you can now find beer cookbooks as well as hundreds of recipes online. The following recipes are examples of how beer can be used for cooking; they include links to their online sources. I have also included some of my own creations. Hopefully, these will inspire you to appreciate another dimension of beer in your own kitchen.

PART I: BEER IN YOUR KITCHEN

Adapted from YourBeerNetwork.com
(December 11, 2011; March 15, 2012; and January 26, 2013)

As you are aware, there is an ongoing but unacknowledged competition between beer and wine—which one is better? Recently, I was asked by a wine snob, "OK, guzzler, if beer is so great, why don't we cook with it?"

TO YOUR HEALTH!

Darn good question, snob. Of course, it is well known that wine contains umami, that elusive savory, protein flavor—the "fifth taste." So adding even a dash of wine enhances the flavor of the most bland stews and vegetable dishes. But try that with beer and the result is often bitter or unpalatable.

Yet beer *does* have a place in our cuisine as an ingredient, in addition to the fact that it is the best accompanying beverage to just about any type of American or ethnic food. (Take that, wine snob!) There are many traditional dishes in which beer is an essential component, such as Welsh rarebit and beef carbonnade. But with the recent popularity of craft beer, many cooks are looking to beer to further enhance their cooking and baking creations.

This chapter is not meant to be a cookbook of recipes using beer, since there are now many good cookbooks that cover this topic, as well as online recipes featuring beer. Instead, it tries to give you an idea of how beer can be used to enhance both traditional and innovative cuisine. I've only included a few recipes that I've used myself, including one that I created for *Pils Noir* ice cream. You can find other recipes online using the links I suggest.

We've established that beer does not have umami, so what does it contribute to our food? It certainly does not bring the same kind of sweetness that wine does, since it contains very little sugar—which is all used up by the yeast. But it does bring a hearty, bread-like quality that adds body to a dish. White ales, wheat beers, and malty German beers do a good job of providing this characteristic, but so do some American ales.

But beware the hops! There's a good reason that we don't routinely use hops as seasoning in our foods. The bitterness of the hop will always overpower its flavor, unless it is carefully balanced with the other seasonings in the dish or even the addition of sugar. Hoppy beers complement red meat best. English bitters and Irish beers have less bitterness (low IBUs) and are great cooking beers. Stouts and porters may contain some sugar, and they have a sweet, mellow quality that works with hearty foods and even desserts.

CHAPTER 7: COOKING WITH BEER

What follows is a brief survey of recipes that use beer as an ingredient. I have included the links so you can feast your eyes and then feast your palate, if you're inclined to try them yourself. At the end of this chapter are four recipes that I have kitchen tested myself and that are now among my favorites.

One of the benefits of cooking with beer is that you get to drink the leftovers. Yes, beer does have a place in your kitchen.

SEAFOOD

Shellfish pairs well with beer—the hoppier the better. There is nothing like an American IPA to drink with lobster, clams, or crab. In addition to drinking the beer, you can use it to steam shrimp, but it will taste better with a lager or a pale ale than with a hoppy IPA. And of course, beer-battered fish-and-chips is a staple food item in many American bars—so use a lager for batter, too. While you're at it, throw in a few onion rings. Used in batter, the carbonation of the beer acts as leavening to keep the batter light.

http://beer.about.com/od/fishshellfish/r/beersteamshrimp.htm
http://allrecipes.com/recipe/beer-batter/

Mussels steamed in Belgian beer. This is my favorite beer recipe. Truly delightful! Mussels are a traditional Flemish dish, which I first tried while touring Normandy by car. It always brings back memories of eating in small seaside villages. A garlic mayonnaise and thin-cut french fries accompany the mussels, and the combination is called *Moules-frites*. The Hopleaf bar, in Chicago, specializes in Belgian beers on draft, and their recipe for beer-steamed mussels uses Belgian witbeer (wheat beer).

http://timeoutchicago.com/restaurants-bars/62736/hopleafs-mussels

Clams. An East Coast variant of Moules-frites uses clams and American wheat beers, such as *Samuel Adams Summer Ale.*

http://www.bostonfoodandwhine.com/2010/08/13/steamed-clams-in-a-beer-lemon-and-garlic-broth/

TO YOUR HEALTH!

MEAT

Pot roast. Beer pairs so well with red meat! That leads us to my second-favorite beer dish, *Guinness* pot roast. This recipe was given to me by one of my patients, who used to serve it on St. Patrick's Day (see chapter 1.) The sweetness of the honey and the sharpness of the fresh basil perfectly balance the hops in the beer. The recipe is at the end of the chapter.

Beef carbonnade. Another Flemish beer-based dish is beef carbonnade, which is the national dish of Belgium. In this hearty beef stew, the hops are moderated by strong seasonings (onion, garlic, thyme, bay leaf) and softened by the addition of brown sugar.

http://frenchfood.about.com/od/soupsandstews/r/flemishbeef-stew.htm

Lamb. Another beer-and-meat favorite is beer-braised lamb shanks. The strong lamb flavor pairs well with an IPA.

http://cookingfortwo.about.com/od/lamb/r/lambshanks.htm

Sausage. And of course, bratwurst just HAS to be cooked in beer, doesn't it? Variations on this recipe cook onions, beer, and brats together, finish the brats on a grill, then serve them in rolls covered with the onion-beer mixture. Great game-day and Super Bowl food.

http://allrecipes.com/recipe/beer-brats/

Chicken. Besides the ubiquitous beer-can chicken, I haven't found many chicken-based beer recipes. The link below suggests an interesting variant in which beer is used as part of the brining solution. I would use a very light lager with this one.

http://www.wikihow.com/Cook-a-Chicken-With-Beer

CHEESE AND BREAD

Beer bread is terribly easy and fun to make, and it's a surprise to serve. The basic recipe consists of flour, sugar, salt, baking powder, and beer. The carbonation in the beer provides additional

CHAPTER 7: COOKING WITH BEER

leavening. There are many variations, depending on the type of beer used and additional ingredients such as cheese, cranberries, nuts, or caraway seeds. My variation is given at the end of the chapter. Use the recipe that I have provided as a starter, add your own variations, and let your imagination run wild.

Welsh rarebit. Another traditional beer dish not often served in this country is Welsh rarebit. Welsh rarebit is a fabulous melted-cheese sauce made with English porter and served over bread. Unlike fondue, it's made with beer, not wine. Take that, wine snobs!

http://www.foodnetwork.com/recipes/alton-brown/welsh-rarebit-recipe/index.html

VEGETABLES

Beer and vegetables are unexplored territory for me, but I am inspired to experiment. When it comes to using beer as flavoring, you have to think strong-flavored vegetables. Brussels sprouts, cabbage, and sauerkraut seem to work well when braised in beer. Going with the stronger flavors and sweet veggies, how about carrots and dill in beer?

http://www.cdkitchen.com/recipes/recs/340/Carrots-In-Beer-And-Dill94221.shtml

Or how about wild mushrooms and leeks cooked in *Stone Levitation Ale*? By the way, the Stone Blog is a great source for creative beer-based recipes.

http://blog.stonebrew.com/?p=2391

DESSERTS

Gingerbread. There is no doubt that porters and stouts are great ingredients for desserts, going well with chocolate cake, brownies, and gingerbread. Milk stouts often contain unfermentable sugar—usually lactose derived from milk—which adds sweetness as well as body. The Gramercy Tavern in New York has apparently been serving beer gingerbread for years. I've seen variations using milk stout or other stouts, but *Guinness* seems to be the favorite brew to use.

http://smittenkitchen.com/2008/12/gramercy-taverns-gingerbread/

***Guinness* chocolate cake.** Chocolate cake made with stout is spectacular, as are brownies and other chocolate desserts made with the same. I made a *Guinness* chocolate cake, and it was a big hit; the recipe is at the end of this chapter. Remember to use good-quality, high-cocoa chocolate, especially for the glaze.

***Guinness* ice cream.** I first discovered beer ice cream when I lived in Boston; around St. Patrick's Day (March 17), *Guinness* ice cream would appear. The confection was made locally and served at many ice cream parlors and taverns. In one variation, a scoop was put in a glass of stout to make an ice cream float. Enjoy!

http://www.yumsugar.com/Guinness-Ice-Cream-Recipe-14829658

Pils Noir *ice cream*. Susquehanna Brewing Co. is a relatively new local brewery. Though it is a small brewery, it is beginning to get noticed for great beer. They give an excellent tour—all you can taste on draft—and also a fine introduction to the ingredients of beer.

On a recent brewery tour, we were given a small bag of malted barley extract. No one was quite sure what to do with the malt extract besides mixing it in chocolate milk (fabulous for chocolate malts). I took this as a challenge to create a new recipe using the malt and decided to develop an ice cream that would feature the flavors of beer. For the taste base, I used the SBC *Pils Noir*, a fine, rich black pilsner hopped with Willamette, Mt. Hood, Washington, and Czech Saaz hops and darkened using Czech decoction mashing.

I cooked the beer over low heat to concentrate the taste and remove the alcohol, which also helped to dissolve the malt. The

CHAPTER 7: COOKING WITH BEER

Golden warm lager bread

ice cream was made in a small hand-crank ice cream maker—it was creamy and delicious, reminiscent of chocolate malt, but with a decidedly adult finish.

So reader, these are the flavors of beer as translated into cuisine. I will leave you to answer the question: which is better, beer or wine?

TO YOUR HEALTH!

PART II: FAVORITE RECIPES

The following is a selection of beer-containing recipes that I've tried. They were either created by me (bread, ice cream), given to me by a friend (pot roast), or adapted from an online variation (chocolate cake). All except the *Guinness* Chocolate Cake were featured on YourBeerNetwork.com.

GUINNESS POT ROAST

YourBeerNetwork.com (February 1, 2012)

- 1½ pounds chuck or round roast (about 1-inch thick and sliced into about 8 pieces)
- 2 medium onions
- 1/2 pound carrots
- 2 heaping tablespoons flour, seasoned with salt and pepper
- 2–3 tablespoons cooking oil
- 1/2 teaspoon fresh basil, minced
- 2/3 cup *Guinness*
- 1 teaspoon honey
- 2/3 cup stock or water
- Salt and pepper to taste

Peel and chop the onions and slice carrots into 1-inch pieces.

Cook the onions in the oil until soft, then layer them in a greased, ovenproof dish.

Roll the beef in some seasoned flour and brown in remaining oil in the pan; remove beef slices as they are cooked and place on top of the onions, in a single layer.

Arrange the carrots around the beef.

Add more oil to the pan as needed, and stir in the remainder of the seasoned flour. Cook for a minute or two, stirring constantly, then add the basil and the *Guinness*.

CHAPTER 7: COOKING WITH BEER

Allow to boil for a minute or two, stirring constantly, then add the honey and the stock. Return to a boil and pour over the meat.

Cover and cook in the oven at 325 degrees for 1½ hours.

PILS NOIR ICE CREAM
YourBeerNetwork.com (December 11, 2011)

- 1/2 cup *Pils Noir* beer, Susquehanna Brewing Company (or any dark and lightly hopped beer, such as a German bock)
- 1/4 cup sugar
- 2 heaping tablespoons dried malt extract (brewing ingredient) (If not available, use honey or brown sugar.)
- 1½ cups heavy cream
- 2 medium organic eggs, lightly beaten
- 1/8 teaspoon salt

Mix the beer and sugar in a deep saucepan; heat to dissolve sugar.

Cook on very low heat until the volume is reduced by half, then slowly stir in the malt extract. Give it time to dissolve! Mix in well, then put the saucepan in the refrigerator until the contents are cool.

Add about half the cream and mix well to completely dissolve the thick, syrupy beer extract.

Transfer to a 2-quart measuring cup and add the eggs and the remainder of the cream, bringing the volume up to 1 pint.

Whirl in a blender (optional step), then transfer to the ice cream freezer and freeze as usual.

Note: for a 1-quart ice cream freezer, double the recipe and use 3 eggs instead of 2.

GOLDEN WARM LAGER BREAD
YourBeerNetwork.com (January 26, 2013)

- 2½ cups plain flour
- 1 tablespoon baking powder
- 2 tablespoons dried malt extract + 1 tablespoon sugar

(Or substitute 2 tablespoons sugar, if malt extract powder is not available.)
1½ teaspoons baking soda
1 teaspoon salt
1 12-ounce bottle lager
(recommended: SBC *Goldencold Lager*)
1 cup shredded cheddar cheese
1–2 teaspoons coarse sea kosher salt (optional)

Preheat oven to 375 degrees.

Grease and flour a 9-inch loaf pan.

Mix all dry ingredients, then stir in beer and cheese until blended.

Spread evenly in pan and sprinkle the coarse salt on top.

Bake 45–55 minutes, until a toothpick comes out clean.

GUINNESS CHOCOLATE CAKE

1 cup (2 sticks) unsalted butter at room temperature
2½ cups all-purpose flour
3/4 teaspoon baking soda
1/2 teaspoon salt
3/4 cup *Guinness* stout
12 ounces semisweet chocolate
(recommend 72% *Ghirardelli*)
3 large eggs
1 cup granulated sugar
1 cup packed dark brown sugar
1/2 cup sour cream
1/2 cup heavy cream

Heat oven to 350. Butter a 12-cup Bundt pan.

In a medium bowl, whisk together the flour, baking soda, and salt.

In a small saucepan, combine the butter and stout. Cook over medium heat, add 8 ounces of the chocolate, and whisk until smooth.

CHAPTER 7: COOKING WITH BEER

With a mixer, beat the eggs and sugars on medium-high until fluffy. Beat in the chocolate mixture and sour cream. Reduce speed to low and gradually mix in the flour mixture until just combined (do not overmix).

Pour into the prepared pan and bake until a toothpick inserted into the center comes out with a few moist crumbs attached, for 45–55 minutes. Let cool 30 minutes, in the pan, then invert onto a rack to cool completely.

Prepare the glaze: In a small saucepan, bring the heavy cream just to a boil. Do not let it get too hot or the chocolate will separate. Remove from the heat, add the remaining 4 ounces of chocolate, and let sit 5 minutes. Whisk until melted and smooth. Drizzle the cake with the glaze and let it set before serving.

CHAPTER 8

OTHER SPIRITS

It's a short step from beer to whiskey—and that step is called distillation. Whiskey—whether scotch, bourbon, or rye—starts with the fermentation of barley, corn, and other grains.

No matter where in the world the whiskey is made, it has its own unique regional character, as does craft beer. You have to spend some time on the peaty island of Islay to fully understand single malt scotch, and bourbon is uniquely American in its history and flavor.

The best way to learn about these spirits, and to appreciate them, is to visit the distilleries and taste their finished products. This chapter is as much about travel as it is about spirits, and it illustrates the *terroir* of fermented grain products.

WHY I DRINK BOURBON, NOT BEER, IN SOUTHERN INDIANA

YourBeerNetwork.com (December 9, 2011)

I was recently posted to Madison, Indiana for two weeks, filling in for a local doctor. It's a small town in southern Indiana, just across the Ohio River from Kentucky. Madison is a unique place. In the 1800s it was the busiest riverboat town on the river—until the big boats became extinct. So its roots are rough, tough, drinkin', and carousin'. That probably explains why there are so many great bars with live music every night, in a town with a population of less than 12,000. I had a great after-hours time there.

CHAPTER 8: OTHER SPIRITS

So why couldn't I get a good draft beer in that town?

Most bars have a few taps, but Madison beer drinkers prefer to quaff the mass-market stuff. The premier beer is *Guinness* (ho hum). My local bartender, Matt, who poured a killer black-and-tan at my local hangout, Joeyg's, said they had no IPAs on draft because they can't give them away. They just never caught on. There is one brewery in town, but it was never open, so I had no chance to taste a local beer. I was afraid I might die of thirst in that town.

Finally, I discovered why I couldn't get a good draft beer in that town: they drink bourbon! Every bar has good bourbon, and many carry premium bottles that are as pricey as good Scotch. (No, they don't drink Scotch here, either. It never caught on.) They sip it straight-up or on the rocks—not as part of a cocktail, just as a fine spirit. I tried it that way and I agree. The better the bourbon, the tastier the drink, and the slower the sipping.

So I made it my business to learn what I could about this spirit, to help refine my taste for it. Madison is just across the bridge from Kentucky. Drive 50 miles south of here and you're in bluegrass country, on the Bourbon Trail. If you have a chance to do so, it's worth the trip. You'll have a great time; learn a lot about bourbon; taste some good ones; and along the way, you'll probably get some good barbecue—the food of choice to go with sippin' whiskey.

One Saturday, Rick and I drove into Kentucky to visit Buffalo Trace and Woodford Reserve distilleries. We had noteworthy tours at both places and a chance to taste some wonderful spirits.

I learned that Bourbon was originally the name of the county in Kentucky that was settled by bootleggers fleeing the revenuers in Pennsylvania during the Whiskey Rebellion of 1791–1794. Bourbon County had wonderful, clear limestone water and land especially suited to growing corn. The "beer"—made with corn, malted barley, and rye—was distilled into a clear spirit, and American ingenuity developed the method of aging it in charred oak barrels.

TO YOUR HEALTH!

Here is the legal definition of bourbon in the United States, as specified by the federal government's Standards of Identity for Distilled Spirits:

It must be produced in the United States.

It must contain at least 51% corn.

It must be aged in new, charred oak barrels (the old barrels are sold to Scotland, France, or Home Depot).

It must be distilled to no more than 160 proof (80% alcohol).

It must be entered into barrel aging at no more than 125 proof (62.5% alcohol).

It must be bottled at 80 proof or more. (This is true for all whiskeys.)

To be called *straight bourbon*, it must be aged at least two years, with no added coloring, flavoring, or other spirits.

If you try a taste comparison, you'll find that the difference between a standard whiskey and a single-barrel, aged bourbon is like the difference between *J&B* and a premium 20-year *Macallan* Scotch—or between *Bud Light* and a craft IPA. There is no comparison.

I believe that bourbon is still evolving: most distillers don't want to make the investment in long aging, which wastes time and loses precious volume. But I predict that when the bourbon producers finally realize that a good barrel gets better and commands a much higher price after long aging—as the Scotch distillers recognized a few decades ago—we'll start to see some great stuff. A few forward-looking distilleries are now releasing well-aged bourbons; for example, *Pappy Van Winkle's* released highly prized 20- and 23-year bottles. Keep your eyes peeled for select cask-aged bourbons; though pricey, they make for a real treat.

Thank you, Madison, Indiana, for introducing me to life in a river town. Madison has a slow, relaxed lifestyle, a bit behind the times. And when it comes to liquor trends, this town is so far behind that it's ahead of the curve. I predict that premium bourbon will be "the next big thing" in alcoholic spirits. But for now, back to my beer. I'll have the IPA, thank you.

CHAPTER 8: OTHER SPIRITS

ADDENDUM
The last day in town, I discovered a great restaurant with a very respectable draft list. The 605 Grille has eight taps and a 25-ounce sampler. Noteworthy on their draft list was Upland Brewery's *Komodo Dragonfly*, a very, very black IPA, brewed in nearby Bloomington, Indiana.

BOURBON AND THE DERBY

YourBeerNetwork.com (August 8, 2012)

They say it is the calcium-rich water that strengthens the horses, flavors the bourbon, and colors the grass blue. That is why horse racing and bourbon are inseparable in the bluegrass country of Kentucky. Many Kentucky distilleries pay homage to the thoroughbreds with special bottlings and labels, and Blanton's tops their bottle cork with a horse! But the greatest celebration of this synergy comes with the Kentucky Derby, which takes place at Churchill Downs in Louisville, Kentucky, each year in May.

I watched the Derby this year, along with 15 million other Americans. And like many of them, I enjoyed a few sips of Kentucky bourbon along with the race. It was a good time to take stock of my bourbon collection and share a few sips with my readers.

If you are a reader of YourBeerNetwork.com, you are no doubt a fan of craft beers; you are also probably a connoisseur of fine spirits, such as single malt Scotch, which, after all, is merely distilled beer. You may also enjoy fine wines, cognac, or brandy. But chances are that you don't know much about Kentucky bourbon.

Bourbon is easy to dismiss as unworthy of your attention, since it is a domestic product, readily available, usually mediocre, and inexpensive. Yet when you taste a truly excellent small-batch or handcrafted bourbon, you will discover a unique taste sensation. Good bourbon is a delight, and it is truly an American creation.

TO YOUR HEALTH!

You may recall that I became a fan of Kentucky bourbon when I spent a few weeks on a job in Madison, Indiana, visiting bluegrass country, just across the Ohio river. (See the story above). Since then I have been on the lookout for good bourbon. I buy it when I find it, because small-batch bourbon is just that—there are a limited number of bottles produced, and when it's gone ... well, it's gone. Fortunately, Kentucky bourbon is relatively inexpensive, and even the special-reserve bottlings go for one-third to one-half the cost of comparable single malt Scotches. So I've been able to keep up a nice collection and expand my tastes without spending a fortune.

The stopper on a bottle of Blanton's *single-barrel bourbon, featuring a horse and jockey along with a letter. There are eight unique stoppers that spell "Blanton's."*

CHAPTER 8: OTHER SPIRITS

My husband, Rick, says all small-batch bourbon tastes the same. To some extent, that is true—the predominant tastes are limited by the legal definition of the spirit, consisting of the taste of the distillate itself and the flavors acquired in the aging process. The mash must contain at least 51% corn (the rest can be barley, wheat, or rye); it must be distilled to no more than 160 proof; and it must be aged at least two years in new charred-oak barrels. Unlike beer, there can be no added flavors, such as hops or fruit, and unlike malt Scotch, there is no steeping over peaty fires or sherry-cask aging.

So the only variables are the grain mix and the aging process. Yet within these limits, there is a world of tastes, albeit subtle to the inexperienced palate. Yes, there is a predominant bourbon flavor, but the grain mix changes the background flavor—corn provides the bourbon taste, rye adds pepper, wheat adds sweetness, and barley softens. But aging provides the individualism in color, smoothness, and mouthfeel; aging develops the subtle flavors, such as vanilla, cherry, tannins, maple syrup, tobacco, orange, butterscotch—you name it.

In general, the longer the liquor ages, the more character it develops: the complexity evolves, flavors increase in intensity, and harshness decreases. Even more remarkable is the fact that each barrel in a given lot develops individually with its own characteristics, so that you might find an occasional barrel with exceptional flavor. It takes an experienced taster and master blender to get the uniformity that is expected in some mass-produced bourbon while picking select casks for small-batch bottling.

There is only a handful of Kentucky distilleries, and they produce both mass-market bourbons (*Jim Beam, Four Roses*, etc.) and small-batch bottlings as well as contracting with small producers to distill and age their own individual mix. But the number of small-batch bourbon distilleries is growing around the country as bourbon's popularity increases.

So let's start tasting my collection of Kentucky bourbons, as it existed on Derby Day. Before we start, remember that these spirits are for sipping, not for shots. Sip them neat to get the maximum aroma and flavor intensity, or enjoy them my favorite way—in a tumbler over ice—which softens and smoothens the taste.

We'll start with *Maker's Mark*, which is packaged with the familiar red wax seal on the cork. Many of us were introduced to small-batch bourbons with this brand, now readily available in most bars. *Maker's* is bottled at 90 proof (45% ABV) and is aged seven and a half years. It has a high proportion of wheat in the mix, giving it a sweet flavor profile. It has been described as like buttery toast or syrupy, so it's likely to be a good breakfast drink (just kidding). *Maker's* is a bit harsh on its own, compared to some of the others, but it is a good mixer for Manhattans and whiskey sours if you're not ready for straight whiskey.

Basil Hayden's, aged eight years, is a good choice for a "starter" small-batch bourbon. It exemplifies the classic bourbon flavor and is mild, very smooth, and lower in alcohol than most other whiskies (80 proof, 40% ABV). It has twice as much rye as most others, giving it a honey and peppery taste. *Basil Hayden's* costs about the same as *Maker's Mark*, and I feel it's a bit easier to drink and enjoy on its own. Though not particularly distinguished, there is nothing wrong with it, either.

On the other end of the spectrum, we have *Bookers*, aged seven years, bottled at a hefty 65% ABV! This bourbon, produced by Jim Beam, is uncut, unfiltered, straight from the barrel, and bottled at its natural proof. It has an oaky vanilla aroma and an intense fruit-and-tannin taste with a long finish. I was introduced to it in a short glass over ice by a bartender in bluegrass country who said it was his favorite drink. It has become mine, too. This is a very sophisticated drink, not for the faint of heart nor for the short of cash. The long finish stays on your palate forever, so you can sip this drink slowly for hours. Very pleasurable indeed.

Blanton's is the one with the horse on the cork. It is a *single-barrel* bourbon, which means that each bottling comes from only one select barrel that is numbered and signed—you can tell exactly what batch and barrel it came from, if you care to know (and some people do). The aging time varies since it's harvested when it's ready, not by the clock. This excellent bourbon is pro-

CHAPTER 8: OTHER SPIRITS

duced by Buffalo Trace distillery, which also makes the small-batch standard *Buffalo Trace* (a uniform-tasting small batch is mixed from a number of barrels). *Blanton's* is very pleasant, smooth with an up-front taste of caramel and vanilla, but not long on the finish. If you are really into it, you can collect all eight different horses!

Eagle Rare is also produced by Buffalo Trace Distillery and is my absolute all-around favorite—possibly one of the best values in Kentucky bourbon. It's a very affordable 10-year-old single-barrel, 90 proof bourbon (45% ABV). It has oaky vanilla flavors and is as smooth as silk. Not a harsh note in the bottle.

I stumbled upon *Black Maple Hill "Limited Edition"* unexpectedly, at the Pennsylvania State Liquor Store. This is a small-batch bottling from Heaven Hill Distilleries, at 95 proof. There is a lot of wheat in the mash, resulting in a very sweet distillate. The flavor is unique, with a lot of fruit characteristics, and reviewers have variously tasted black cherry, butterscotch, peppermint, coconut—and jelly beans?

Jefferson's Presidential Select, 17-year (94 proof) bourbon is currently the most "collectable" bourbon in my cabinet. Its claim to fame is that it is aged in Stitzel-Weller barrels, the same ones used for the legendary *Pappy Van Winkle's* bourbon. (I say "legendary" because *Pappy Van Winkle's* is produced in such small amounts that it is almost impossible to purchase!)

This is an exceptionally good select barrel that is very intense and has a much stronger aroma than anything else in my collection. It's comparable to a good Highland malt whiskey. It has unexpected floral notes, very mellow flavor, and a long, long finish. It's aged almost twice as long as most of the other single-barrels I have found. It costs twice as much, too, and I'm not sure that it's twice as good, but it's really very, very nice. It is fun to bring out for guests who appreciate well-aged spirits. The *Pappy Van Winkle's* was considerably better, but that's long gone.

By the time you read this piece, the Derby will be long forgotten, and my bourbon collection will probably look very different. But I hope these little tastes served as an introduction to the fine bourbons of Kentucky and inspired you to try a few or even make the trip to bluegrass country to visit the Churchill Downs racetrack and stop in to a few distilleries. You're always welcome to visit!.

THE BEST LITTLE WHISKEY BAR IN TEXAS

YourBeerNetwork.com (April 5, 2013)

If you have time to visit only one bar in Houston, skip the beer bars and go directly to Reserve 101. This is the best whiskey bar in Texas and among the best in the world, rated "Gold" by *Whiskey Magazine*.

This unpretentious venue in downtown Houston has over 200 bottles of great whiskey, with a continuously rotating stock. The knowledgeable bartenders are happy to assist you in selecting something that suits your tastes, from Irish and Scotch whiskey to bourbon, rye, and other spirits. Unlike the custom and practice at a beer bar, you won't be offered a taste at a whiskey bar, but at Reserve 101, you will have the opportunity to sniff the "angel's share" (aroma) to help make your selection.

We were lucky to sit at the bar and meet one of the owners, Mike Raymond, who has a clear vision of what a good whiskey bar should be—inspired in part by our favorite Chicago haunt, Delilah's. Mike Miller, the owner of Delilah's, picked out a selection of his favorites for Rick and me to taste; Miller has over 500 bottles at Delilah's, whereas Raymond has about half that many at Reserve 101. However, both have the same funky-punk but serious ambiance that I have grown to associate with high-end spirits bars.

On to the drink. Rick stuck to Scotch and I worked on American bourbons, with assistance from my daughter. I didn't take notes, but among the great spirits we tasted were the following:

CHAPTER 8: OTHER SPIRITS

Scotch:

Lagavulin 21-year: This was an OMG! both in taste and in dollars per shot.

Yamizaki 12- and 18-year: The 12-year is a much better value, but the 18 is smoother.

Bourbon:

Cyrus Noble, a Kentucky bourbon mixed in San Francisco

High West Double Rye

Angel's Envy special blend, mixed by the proprietor, Mike Raymond. This is a unique Kentucky-style bourbon that is finished in sherry. Raymond improved on this by producing his own private bottling, which mixed three batches to his specs, with a sublime result. This one is worth a trip to Houston to try.

So make a point of visiting this bar if you are in Houston. And for that matter, if you visit only one rodeo this year—get to Houston's. It's the best. We spent a day there watching cattle roping, mutton busting, and bronco riding; trying on cowboy gear; eating barbecue and corn dogs; and drinking awful beer.

Which brings me to the subject of beer. Houston is not what I would call a beer town. For its size, it has only a few well-established microbreweries, with Karbach Brewing Co. being the new kid on the block. Admittedly, I did not have time to explore Houston beers, but my overall impression is that these folks are lager lovers. That's possibly because the big three of Houston cooking—Tex-Mex, barbecue, and Gulf seafood—go well with lagers, especially the usual Mexican imports.

Shiner Bock is the local beer staple, and it's good. I also found two ales on draft—Fireman's *#4 Blonde Ale* and St. Arnold's *Amber Ale*—and they were both good, pairing well with food. They were underhopped to my palate, tasting rather like lagers, without the citrus punch I prefer. Karbach's lineup seems to be leaning toward hoppier beers, and perhaps next time, I'll find some to try. I'd love to hear my readers' opinions on Texas beers.

TO YOUR HEALTH!

FOR PEAT'S SAKE: SINGLE MALT SCOTCH

YourBeerNetwork.com (October 8, 2013)

Most craft beer lovers enjoy single malt Scotch, which is another form of fermented malted barley. Like craft beer, Scotch has great snob appeal, because you can analyze it, compare tasting notes, and show off your expertise. And single malt Scotch is the epitome of delightfully snobby drinks because developing a refined palate takes time, commitment, money—and (if you're lucky) travel.

You don't have to visit Scotland to appreciate fine Scotch, but it certainly helps, because among the spirits of the world, nothing is more evocative of place than single malt Scotch whiskey. It truly *tastes* like Scotland. And of the single malts, none can top the Islay malts, which are the peatiest—and most reminiscent of Scotland.

I have been to Scotland at least four times; all the visits involved Scotch tasting (snob appeal), but the most remarkable visit was to Islay (pronounced *eye-lay*). Islay is an island in the southern Hebrides, on the west coast of Scotland. It is made entirely of peat formed from the mud and vegetation of ancient moors, resting on a pile of limestone rock in the Atlantic. It is a starkly beautiful place, with rocky shores and windswept fields, where few trees can survive the harsh weather.

Along the coast are the towns of Port Charlotte, Bowmore, Port Askaig, and Bridgend. In the interior are farms where they grow barley and wheat, and where they raise sheep and the distinctive-looking Highland cattle, with their long red hair. The farms are dotted with white stone cottages, with peat smoke rising from chimneys. Peat smoke is everywhere, and after a week on the island, the smoke permeates your very clothes. You will never forget the scent. Peat is used for heating, in cheerful fireplaces in the pubs, and to smoke the malted barley used to make Scotch.

CHAPTER 8: OTHER SPIRITS

Rick and I spent a week in this remote place at a quaint bed-and-breakfast situated on a working farm on the ocean. We relaxed, visited the few local sights, and drank as much single malt as possible. This small island (only 600 square miles) houses eight working distilleries; we managed to visit six of them and tasted Scotch from all of them.

Here in Islay, Scotch is made from malted barley that's smoked over Islay peat, mashed with pure water from Islay streams, and then distilled. The distillate is aged in used oak barrels imported from bourbon distilleries in the United States. Because the spirits remain in oak from 8 to over 20 years, there are large storage warehouses throughout the island where the pretax spirit is carefully guarded under lock and key. Some warehouses hold barrels from distilleries that have long since closed, and those carry a premium price tag (since they aren't made anymore!).

The increased demand for Islay Scotch has been accommodated by importing some barley from the mainland and by establishing a malting works in Port Ellen to handle the overflow; however, to maintain the distinctive taste and high quality of the Scotch, only Islay peat is used, and the distilleries source water from their own sites. Each water source is unique. Usually, it's an open stream containing variable amounts of limestone, rust-tinged stone, and peat. And Islay peat is unique among peats of the world—strong and smoky, almost piney, with some taste of the ocean as well.

The reason to go to Islay, of course, is to learn about malt Scotch, taste it, and visit the distilleries. All are in beautiful settings, most of them overlooking the ocean and having a comfortable tasting room. All peaty Scotches are similar, but there are subtle distinctions among them, which you will soon appreciate after spending a week tasting all of them. As a cask ages, the peatiness declines, while other flavors mature and add character. Each of the eight distilleries has its own recognizable flavor, from the extreme malts of the south shore (found at Lagavulin, Laphroaig and Ardbeg) to the gentlest extremes of the north (at Bunnahabhain and Caol Ila).

TO YOUR HEALTH!

If you have time for only one distillery tour when visiting Islay, make sure to get to Lagavulin. With luck, you can attend a Scotch tasting hosted by Iain McArthur, an Islay native who has been a warehouseman at the distillery for over 40 years. He will teach you about tasting fine Scotch and will allow you to sample some of Lagavulin's more exclusive old barrels. If you can't get to Scotland, watch his tour on YouTube at http://www.youtube.com/watch?v=ro3HKp_pOwM, and listen to his delightful Islay burr. It is an unforgettable experience.

Scotch aging in oak barrels at Lagavulin.

Laphroaig also has an excellent tour. If you want to understand peat, you have to visit this one. This distillery makes the peatiest Scotch in the world. They do their own floor malting and peat-smoke it on site. You are even invited to add a chunk of peat to the smoker and become part of the process. The Laphroaig tour has a fine tasting experience, and as a bonus, you can become a "Friend of Laphroaig," which entitles you to a lifetime lease on a square foot of the Laphroaig lands, through which runs their all-important water source, the Kilbride stream.

You don't have to visit Laphroaig to become a "Friend" and claim your plot of land; you can do it online if you have

CHAPTER 8: OTHER SPIRITS

purchased a bottle of their malt. Just visit www.laphroaig.com/friends. However, you will need to visit the distillery to collect your "rent," which is a small, TSA-friendly-sized bottle of Scotch to take home.

Like many Islay distilleries, Ardbeg was established in the 1700s. However, it couldn't make a go of it in the 20th century and closed in the 1980s. It has reopened and recently released a delightful 10-year, very peaty malt. The distillery is also bottling whiskey that it purchased when it reopened. Some of that whiskey is over 40 years old and has the highest ratings (and the highest prices—some over $1,000 per bottle).

Similarly, Bruichladdich went fallow but was subsequently purchased by a group of private investors in 2000. They are also releasing the bottlings of their *Legacy* Scotches, from 30- to 40-year-old casks, to lofty reviews and even loftier prices. Their new production releases are not as highly rated, but few casks have had enough time to mature yet.

Bowmore is situated in the town of the same name, on the shore of Loch Indaal. It is one of the bigger distilleries. Established in 1779, it is now owned by Suntory, and that is probably why it has a corporate feel to it. Bowmore produces a great deal of Scotch, most of which is consistently good and is described as "smoky" rather than "peaty."

Kilchoman is the first distillery to be built on the island in 124 years and is reviving the tradition of farm distilling, having all parts of the process—growing barley, malting, distilling, maturing, and bottling—carried out on Islay. It began production in July 2005 and released its first 100-percent Islay whiskey in 2011, which explains why we didn't taste it during our 2010 trip. The releases have gotten fairly good reviews, considering how short they have been aged. I haven't tasted any yet.

Finally, the Northern distilleries, Caol Ila and Bunnahabhain. Sadly, we ran out of time on our trip—we'll leave those for you to taste. You, too, can become a Scotch snob.

AFTERWORD

When the first posts on YourBeerNetwork.com were published in January 2011, craft beer was neither understood nor widely appreciated. To most Americans at the time, beer was a ubiquitous alcoholic beverage, produced by one of a few large brand names, drunk from a can or bottle, and not particularly distinguished. To some of us, though, beer was a delightful drink, whether it be an imported English bitter, a German pilsner, a Belgian abbey ale, or one of the newly emerging craft beers. It was a nice change to drink an American beer that was as good as the quality imports.

We staff writers—beer bloggers—for YourBeerNetwork.com were novices, but we learned as we tasted and as we wrote, keeping one step ahead of our readership. We did our research online and at breweries. We made friends with brewers and bartenders. We insisted that our beer be served in a glass, not from the bottle. We reviewed beers and restaurants that served good beer, and we paired beer with food. We patronized restaurants and pubs that served quality beer, and we avoided the others—and we let the managers know how we felt. We encouraged our readers to do the same.

At first I was content to share my yarns and travel stories and to write about the local breweries and the regional customs of Northeastern Pennsylvania. But as the months passed, I began to recognize what a national treasure we had in American craft beers. I wanted to get the word out. I was now on a mission to educate people about craft beer and to promote it.

Our voice was heard. Craft beer has been steadily gaining in popularity—in part because of the efforts of sites like ours. Food and drink writers have discovered it, brewfests have sprung up around the country, discerning restaurants now feature beer pairings, and neighborhood bars now serve craft beer on draft. Brewpubs and microbrewery tasting rooms have begun

BY CAROL A. WESTBROOK, MD, PHD

to appear in many communities. Previously hard to find, craft beer has become an established part of the American food and drink scene in just three years.

If we look back at brewing history in the United States, we realize that this is not a new trend; rather, we are going back to our historical roots. Many people date the start of the craft beer movement to 1969, when Fritz Maytag bought Anchor Brewing Co. in San Francisco. But as a matter of fact, we have always been a craft beer nation, because most of the beer we drank was produced in small breweries and drunk locally—at least until prohibition.

The number of breweries in the United States hit an all-time high in 1873, with over 4,000 breweries—two-thirds more than are operating today! Yet only a hundred years later, in 1983, there were only 80 breweries. If you're old enough to remember the beers we drank in the eighties—well, they weren't memorable, were they?

What happened to all of those breweries? A number of factors combined to close them or encourage them to sell out to the big guys. These included Prohibition; refrigeration, which allowed for wider distribution; the development of brewing techniques that favored large-scale production; and the aggressive business practices of the big brewing companies. By 1980, the top six breweries (Anheuser-Busch, Miller, Heileman, Stroh, Coors, and Pabst) controlled 92 percent of beer production. Even today, the two largest, Anheuser-Busch InBev and MillerCoors, control over 75 percent of the U.S. beer industry.

But now, thanks to the craft beer movement, the number of small breweries is on the increase, and those breweries are commanding an increasing market share of beer production—which is now over 10 percent and growing every year. The number of craft breweries has been increasing at a rate of almost one per day, as supply can barely keep up with demand. As of June 2013, there were 2,483 small breweries in the United States, including brewpubs, microbreweries, and regional breweries—as compared to 24 large, noncraft breweries.

The larger brewing companies have taken notice. They are now producing more beer that appeals to the micro-lover's palate, such as InBev's *Shock Top* and MillerCoors's *Blue Moon*. They are also acquiring craft breweries, as happened with MillerCoors's acquisition of Leinenkugel and Budweiser's (now InBev's) acquisition of Goose Island Brewery. Technically, these can no longer be called *craft* breweries, even though the beer they make may look and taste similar to their original brews.

I believe that competition in the beer world is a good thing because it keeps the standards higher. Why settle for mediocrity when we could be drinking better-tasting beer made with higher-quality ingredients? Of course there will always be a demand for a cold *Bud*, a *Coors Lite*, or a *PBR* drunk from the can or bottle. These are an undeniable part of our heritage. I can't imagine going to a ballgame without downing a cold beer or watching the Super Bowl without a spectacular *Budweiser* commercial.

But I do try to avoid the craft beer look-alikes, because I feel that we, as consumers, must continue the demand for *true* craft beer—or we may end up back in 1980.

A craft brewery, by definition, is small and independent, and it brews traditional, all-malt beers. When you purchase a regional craft beer over a mass-market international brand, you are buying local. You are providing jobs and encouraging the success of small-business entrepreneurs. You are helping to keep your local microbrewery or brewpub from closing due to lack of business or from being acquired by InBev or MillerCoors.

But most importantly, you are ensuring a continuing supply of the highest-quality beer, made with the best ingredients, to enrich your life and help you enjoy good times.

And that, after all, is what this book is about. To your health!

TO YOUR HEALTH!

ABOUT THE AUTHOR

Dr. Carol A. Westbrook was born and raised in Chicago, Illinois, and studied at the University of Chicago, where she received her MD and PhD degrees. She has over 20 years of faculty experience at three medical schools—doing clinical care, research, and teaching—and is the author of 100 scholarly papers. She also holds a patent for leukemia diagnosis. She is now in private practice as a medical oncologist in Wilkes-Barre, Pennsylvania.

Dr. Westbrook's column, *The Beer Clinic*, has been a regular feature of YourBeerNetwork.com since the site began in 2011. She is also a contributing writer for 3QuarksDaily.com's *Monday Magazine*, in which she writes a bimonthly feature about health, science—and occasionally, beer. An experienced public speaker, Dr. Westbrook has appeared on numerous local TV shows and at community events discussing cancer research and treatment. Her first book, *Ask an Oncologist*, is a helpful guide for cancer patients and their caregivers.

In her spare time, Dr. Westbrook volunteers her services at the Care and Concern free clinic in Pittston, Pennsylvania. Other interests include running, home brewing, and traveling with her husband, Rick Rikoski. She divides her time between Wilkes-Barre and Beverly Shores, Indiana, where she lives with her husband.

Made in the USA
Lexington, KY
05 February 2018